Made for Life
Coping, competence and cognition

Made for Life

Coping, competence and cognition

Johanna Turner

METHUEN

LONDON and NEW YORK

First published in 1980 by
Methuen & Co. Ltd
11 New Fetter Lane, London EC4P 4EE

Published in the USA by
Methuen & Co.
in association with Methuen, Inc.
733 Third Avenue, New York, NY 10017

© 1980 Johanna Turner

Typeset by Red Lion Setters, Holborn, London
Printed in Great Britain by
Richard Clay (The Chaucer Press) Ltd
Bungay, Suffolk

British Library Cataloguing in Publication Data
Turner, Johanna
Made for life.
1. Emotions in children
2. Affect (Psychology)
3. Cognition in children
I. Title
155.4′22   BF723.E6   80-40330
ISBN 0-416-72690-9 ✓
ISBN 0-416-72700-X Pbk
(University paperback 712)

To
Matthew Forster

Contents

Acknowledgements

This book has been written during part of a sabbatical year, granted by the University of Sussex for writing and research. I am most grateful for this. I would like to thank my colleagues for their helpful comments and criticisms and in particular Mr Peter Lattin, and Dr Barbara Lloyd for reading portions of the manuscript and for helping me to clarify my ideas. All omissions and inadequacies of treatment are my own. I am particularly aware of the debt I owe to the school and university students who, by sharing with me their aspirations and frustrations, made me realise the significance of the individual in learning situations. My thanks are also due to Mrs Peggy Paine for her good humour, patience and accuracy whilst typing, and retyping, the manuscript. The publishers and I would like to thank the following for their permission to quote tables, diagrams and passages in the text: Academic Press for Tables 3.1 and 3.2; *American Child Psychiatry*, Yale University Press for the extract on pp.28-9; The Developmental Sciences Trust for Table 1.1; The Hogarth Press for Figure 3.1; Holt, Rhinehart & Winston for Tables 6.1 and 6.2; W.W. Norton & Company for Figure 3.1; Plenum Publishing for Tables 3.3 and 4.1; *Science* for Table 2.2; John Wiley & Son for Table 1.2.

Introduction

Nurse's Song

When the voices of children are heard on the green,
And laughing is heard on the hill,
My heart is at rest within my breast,
And everything else is still.

Then come home, my children, the sun is gone down,
And the dews of night arise,
Come, come, leave off play, and let us away
Till the morning appears in the skies.

William Blake: *Songs of Innocence*

Nurse's Song

When the voices of children are heard on the green,
And whisp'rings are in the dale,
The days of my youth rise fresh in my mind,
My face turns green and pale.

Then come home, my children, the sun is gone down,
And the dews of night arise;
Your Spring and your day are wasted in play
And your winter and night in disguise.

William Blake: *Songs of Experience*

These two quotations exemplify contrasting views of childhood arising from the previous experiences of the nurses. Although they were both aware that dusk was falling on the green each interpreted this event differently. No amount of intellectual argument could have reconciled their views since the facts were not in dispute. It was their feelings which gave rise to their discrete cognitive appraisals and determined their subsequent response.

Similarly two children entering the same school at the age of five will, theoretically, be in the same situation and be offered the same educational opportunity. Yet if the meaning of the situation is differentially interpreted because of the children's individual feelings about it then it is in no sense the same nor are their opportunities equal. This book, by reviewing clinical, experimental, and observational studies focuses on developmental experiences which are thought to influence a child's subsequent attitude towards learning situations. In particular it is concerned with the origins of individual difference in self-confidence.

At birth every human infant is partly a product of species-specific evolutionary adaptation, hence he* shares a common past with others of the species and yet he has a unique genotype and faces a future which, through cultural influences, will be like that of some other humans and also like that of no other in so far as it is affected by his own individual experience. Through the same evolutionary adaptation the infant is biologically prepared to pay selective attention to those aspects of the environment which will enable him to actualise his species-specific human potential. During the first few years the fundamental systems of physical movement, perception, cognition and affect will develop and differentiate within the context of a particular cultural, social and physical environment. In this book it will be argued that through the interaction of the infant and his environment a person will emerge with responses which are like those of all other humans, like those of some other humans and like those of no other human (Kluckholm, Murray and Schneider, 1971). Thus the child will develop his individual understandings of situations within the context of shared cultural and social meanings.

The dependent human infant who is, comparatively, immature at birth requires a lengthy period of nurturance. Throughout this period he will be both attempting to act upon the outside world and reacting to it. The variety of experiences in infancy and early childhood, their combinations and permutations, lay the foundation for individual variety within the human species in contrast to the uniformity characteristic of species whose infants are more independent at birth and do not need or have a period of comparative security in which skills necessary for subsequent survival can be observed and practised. Human infants are, above

---

*Throughout this book 'he' will be used where appropriate, to mean 'he/she'. The only justification for this is habit.

all, observant, curious and malleable during their lengthy period of immaturity. Indeed there would be little value in such a period were they not.

This book will consider development during the first five years with special reference to experiences which influence the child's belief in himself and hence his approach to the demands of formal learning. Its initial hypothesis is that a child's capacity to learn, to love and to live in the world will be more affected by his self-confidence than it will be by his current abilities and aptitudes. The child's belief in himself is thought to be significantly influenced by both his experience of being able to affect his environment, or efficacy, and the consistency of the environment to which he is exposed. Since all children are adaptable, which is a biological characteristic, they will develop coping strategies which take into account the extent of their previous experiences of efficacy and environmental consistency. The more these strategies are realistically based the more competently will the child conduct himself when faced with new challenges. Such a competent approach will, in turn, lead to mastery of a particular task and the experience of mastery will reinforce the child's sense of efficacy and self-confidence. There is thus an integral link between (1) feelings about efficacy and environmental consistency, (2) coping strategies based on this belief, (3) competence when faced with real-world tasks and (4) self-confidence flowing from success in such tasks. In general Chapters 1, 2 and 3 will consider influences on a child's sense of efficacy and the importance of environmental consistency, Chapters 4 and 5 will concentrate on the development of autonomy and coping strategies and Chapter 6 will focus on influences which are potent at the moment when the child is starting to interact socially with others outside the home and learning how to learn. It will be most concerned with the years between three and five at which the effects of earlier experiences may first become apparent either at nursery school or when entering infant school.

Each chapter will approach this complex developmental process from a slightly different angle in an attempt to build up a composite picture of the interactions involved. Chapter 1 will be concerned with the family unit consisting of a dependent yet active infant, and a mother and father whose role is both to nurture the infant and facilitate his moving from dependence to independence. It will stress the significance for the infant of his initial attempts to influence his environment. Such attempts take place within the context of the original family unit and, in particular, will be influenced by the sensitivity of the adults to an infant's particular needs. Chapter 2 will concentrate on the infant's own contribution to this unit with special reference to his individual temperament and level of motivation, his cognitive development during the first two years, and his early attempts to communicate. It will be argued that, cognitively, infants show more similarity with one another than they do differences whereas they do exhibit individual temperamental traits and levels of motivation. The parents' response to their infant's constellation of individual characteristics is thought to affect both his early view of himself and his subsequent behaviour. Chapter 3 begins with the development of the sense of self, or with the nature of the infant's 'inner world', and it ends with a discussion of affective development since both forms of development are taking place alongside, and interacting with, those discussed in Chapter 2.

Chapter 4 moves from the encapsulated world of the original family unit to consider the influence of the outside world both as something which the infant wishes to explore and as containing unfamiliar adults with whom the infant must interact. In it is discussed the infant's growing realisation that he is separate from his parents: a realisation that causes him both to seek to attach himself to them and to move away from them. Of particular importance at this stage is the parents' response to the 'psychological birth' of the previously wholly dependent infant. Chapter 5 is concerned with the stage when the infant starts to function as an autonomous individual and to exhibit early coping strategies as he begins to act to a limited extent by himself and for himself. Chapter 6 returns to the family unit but, in contrast to Chapter 1, is no longer concerned with it as a biologically based system, strongly influenced by evolutionary adaptation. In this chapter the family is extended to include siblings and is seen as a socialising influence with special reference to its being the place in which the child will be first exposed to intentional, and unintentional, attempts to teach him the skills necessary for life in his culture and society.

When the child enters school, at the age of five, his behaviour will reflect the effect upon him of the various influences discussed in this book and, it is argued, it is only by understanding the nature and result of their interactions that the child's perception of the situation facing him can be sympathetically comprehended and, if need be, modified. The argument presented follows the discrete strands of development which form the plait of individual differential perception and draws upon the case work of clinicians using psychoanalytic concepts, experimental investigations of infants and children, naturalistic observations, and longitudinal studies, since it is believed that these complementary, yet distinct, approaches draw attention to different aspects of the multifaceted human child.

1

The developmental context

Introduction

In order to trace the development of an individual's belief in his own efficacy it is necessary to start by considering the earliest formative influence provided by the infant's immediate family. This chapter will consider biological and social factors which affect the behaviour of this primary interpersonal unit consisting of father, mother and infant.

It is a fact that every person who exists, or has existed, began that existence firstly by being conceived and, secondly, by separating, physically, from the body of a woman. To live means to have been conceived and born. These two processes result in three related individuals: father, mother, and infant. Some mothers die at the moment of birth or shortly afterwards, others give their infants into the care of surrogates and have either no contact or intermittent contact with them in the future, but, generally, mother and infant remain together for a period of months or years. Some fathers leave the mother after conception, others remain with her but play little part in nurturing their infants but, usually, the father has a continuous relationship with both mother and infant. These separate, yet linked, individuals interact from the moment of birth and the nature of their interaction will be affected by the parents' behaviour, by the infant's behaviour and by the context in which it takes place. A reasonable supposition is that the parents' behaviour is a product of both nature, that is biological predisposition, and culture; and that the infant's is a product of nature plus the effects of having experienced a particular intrauterine environment and birth process. The context in which the parent-infant interaction occurs will also vary in response to cultural, social and physical environmental forces. The number of variables introduced by the parents, the infant and the environmental context make individual differences certain, since it is the interplay of regularities and irregularities in interaction and its context which make each human family unit like all other units, like some other units and like no other unit.

It is often said that the nature of this first interactive relationship will affect the infant's subsequent behaviour. The strength and extent of this effect is disputed, but three points can be made. Firstly, initial exposure to any situation of stimulus is likely to have an enduring effect, and the feelings aroused will remain unless they are modified by the experience of subsequent exposures to similar stimuli. Obviously if no subsequent exposures are experienced, either because they do not occur naturally, or because they are avoided, then the initial reaction will remain intact. In this case long-lasting effects will be found. Secondly, if the infant's response to the initial stimulus is reinforced when he exhibits it on subsequent occasions then this response will strengthen and become a permanent feature of his behaviour. Thirdly, if the infant's initial response is modified by the way he is handled or if he becomes familiar with an originally strange stimulus then his response will alter and long-term effects will not occur (see also p. 31).

Therefore the process of birth initiates an interactive relationship which contains elements common to all family units and elements unique to a particular unit. It is also believed to affect the development of the infant to a certain extent. It is necessary, then, to discover the primary characteristics of this interactive relationship and their effects on infant development.

Infancy: a comparative perspective

One way of approaching parent-infant interaction is via Tinbergen's (1951) four questions. When faced with any piece of behaviour one can ask:

1 What is its immediate causation?
2 How is it related to individual development (ontogeny)?
3 What function has that behaviour in helping the organism to survive?
4 What is its evolutionary history (phylogeny)?

Questions 3 and 4 are the most general and can, usefully, be considered first. The evolutionary approach to human infancy seeks to discover whether there are common patterns in parent-infant behaviour which are adapted to aid survival, the extent to which these behavioural potentials can be said to be biologically 'built in' and whether they can be altered by environmental pressures. Such an approach concentrates upon general behavioural principles which hold for species of different phylogenetic levels, on specific behaviours exhibited by closely related species which may be the result of their common evolutionary history and on similarities between distantly related species caused by exposure to similar selection pressures.

One major, biologically based, difference apparent in infants is between *altricial* and *precocial* development. Precocial development requires the infant to be able to move within minutes or hours of birth, whereas altricial development is characterised by a lengthy period in which the infant is unable to follow its parents and is therefore dependent on them to keep it in a safe place or to carry it. In mammals we find precocial prey and altricial predators. For example preyed-upon animals, such as deer and sheep, are characterised by living in herds or flocks with young who are able to keep up with the group soon after birth. The young are larger and more mature at birth than are the young of predators who have a, potentially, safer infancy. An infant likely to be preyed upon needs to be able to watch out for predators, hence its eyes are placed on the side of its head, its ears are erect and able to move, giving increased acuity. Predator infants must learn to explore their environment to seek out their prey. Initially they show more curiosity and their longer period of dependent, yet safer, infancy enables them both to explore and play.

Non-human primate infants, who represent a species closely related to our own, show many altricial characteristics although they are not predators. They are helpless and dependent at birth and yet are able to obtain care from their biological mothers and others. It appears that the mother becomes predisposed to respond in a particular way to her infant during her pregnancy. Rosenblum and Youngstein (1974) reported a study by Tinkelpaugh and Hartman (1930) which demonstrated the development of this maternal responsiveness. In their study a primate mother, who was due to give birth in three weeks' time, was put with another mother who was just about to give birth. When the infant was born the first mother showed no interest. However when she, herself, was within three days of giving birth they again put her with a mother who was just about to have her infant. This time the first mother showed considerable interest in the infant and the birth process − even to the extent of eating a portion of the placenta. In Rosenblum and Youngstein's own study of rhesus macaques it was found that the macaque mother would deliver her infant and place it against her abdomen. She would then pass the placenta and eat it. They commented that even in those early moments,

> one can observe the first dimensions of the infant's capacity to elicit differential solicitude on the part of the mother. Two objects, smelling and tasting apparently alike, are emitted in rapid succession from the birth canal. One is immediately clutched to the breast, the other immediately consumed. (p. 143)

This maternal responsiveness to her infant appears to continue throughout the dependent period and, in some species, into adolescence.

Lawick-Goodall's (1971) studies of chimpanzees in their natural habitat in Tanzania have provided many insights into mother-infant interaction in the wild. These chimpanzee mothers kept their infants close to them for the first few months, preventing their interaction with others in the troup. At the end of this period the infants extended their social contacts but continued to ride on their mothers' backs until they were aged three or four. Nor were they fully weaned until this time although they started to eat solid foods at about two years. After weaning they maintained close contact with their mothers until adolescence. A noted characteristic of maternal behaviour was the rarity of punishment and the frequency of grooming or tickling as a distractor when the young chimpanzee was exhibiting undesirable behaviours.

During their dependent infancy, curiosity, exploration and play are behaviour characteristics of these primate infants. Such behaviours, which have an evolutionary history, could be expected to occur regularly among members of the species. There are, however considerable differences within species which illustrate, even in a non-human context, the interactive nature of parental behaviour, infant behaviour and environmental context. For example, Kaufman and Rosenblum (1966) made an extensive laboratory study of two types of rhesus macaques: pigtails and bonnets. They were found to differ considerably both in their adult behaviour and in their infant-rearing techniques (Table 1.1). The bonnets were characterised by living in close physical proximity, which involved considerable interaction, whereas the pigtails preferred a more solitary existence and only interacted when grooming, mating or fighting. Adults in both groups showed interest in newborn infants but the pigtail mothers, although solicitous for their infants, remained alone with them and rejected the advances of other adults. The bonnet mothers, on the other hand, shared their infants with other adults in the troup and allowed interaction between infants and other adults from the moment of birth.

Table 1.1 *Comparison of Bonnet and Pigtail normative development and manifestations of infant attachment* (From Rosenblum, 1971)

Behaviour	Bonnets	Pigtails
Gregariousness	High	Low
Maternal protection	Low	High
Infant interaction with adults	High	Low
Peer-play	High	Low
Maternal rejection	Low	High
Response to birth of sibling	Minimal	Disturbance
Cohesiveness of family units	Low	High
Response to maternal loss	Brief agitation (adoption)	Depression

The behaviour of the males towards the infants also differed in the two groups. In the laboratory, adult bonnet males were seen to hold and carry infants (Kaufman and Rosenblum, 1969), whereas in the wild they avoided infants for the first six weeks when the infant's coat still had its neonatal colour (Simonds, 1974). They would, however, if necessary, protect infants (Sugiyama, 1971). In the laboratory the pigtail males showed no sign of caring for or playing with the infants but, in one case, when the mothers had been removed from the group, an adult male protected the motherless infants when they appeared to be in danger (Kaufman and Rosenblum, 1969).

Once the infants began to take the initiative and move away from their mothers the pigtails' mothers retrieved them more frequently and the infants wandered less, whereas the bonnet mothers allowed much greater freedom to their infants, who appeared to take advantage of this. Bonnet mothers were also found to wean earlier and punish less. Both types of infants played to a similar extent but their preferred form of play varied. Pigtail infants exhibited more 'exercise' play – i.e. solitary activities – but the bonnets engaged more in social play with their peers. Following from these observations Kaufman (1974) argued that

> In the mothers' behaviour and the infants' development, we may see a mechanism of great consequence in the perpetuation of the species – characteristic difference in spatial patterning and temperament. Since the difference between these species undoubtedly arose in response to selective pressures, it is reasonable to assume that this difference is genetically encoded. Yet we can see how it becomes realized

ontogenetically under the influence of differential mothering patterns of behaviour. This may be another example of nature's redundancy in ensuring selected patterns of behaviour. As Washburn and Hamburg (1965) put it, 'learning is part of the adaptive pattern of a species, and evolution through selection has built the biological base so that the proper behaviours for that species are the ones that are easily learned.' (pp. 56-7)

Having seen the differential effects of maternal treatment on infant behaviour in a closely related, but non-human, species it is now necessary to continue the comparative picture of infancy by considering a human society which shows considerable cultural differences from our own. Between man's separation from the non-human primates and the development of agriculture (approximately ten thousand years ago) a period of at least 5,000,000 years passed. During that period the hunter/gatherer societies evolved and existed for an extended period in which mother/infant behaviour grew and changed. Today their environment is closer to that of 'evolutionary adaptedness' (Bowlby, 1969) than is our own. That is, its inhabitants live in a type of natural environment similar in some ways to that which our species adapted during its phylogenetic history. Devore and Konner (1974) have studied the !Kung San, who live in Botswana on the north-western edge of the Kalahari Desert, as exemplars of the hunter/gatherer way of life. These people do still exhibit certain behavioural patterns which, having been found to be adaptive, have not been changed.

However, to study the San is not to study 'living relics of our own past' (Devore and Konner, 1974, p. 116):

> The San of the Kalahari Desert are fully modern, psychologically and physically, and their behaviour and institutions have continued to evolve in parallel to those of people around them. One finds among them the full range of human emotional and intellectual potential. Our interest in this people, then, is not that of the entomologist who discovers an extinct insect perfectly preserved in amber, but an interest in the degree to which they represent universally human behavioural responses to the hunter gatherer way of life.

The adult !Kung San were found to be well nourished, had long lives and plenty of leisure. Their search for food was continual but successful, with the women gathering 50-60 per cent of the food in the form of vegetables and, especially, nuts, and the men hunting for meat. !Kung mothers would give birth to an infant every four or five years and although they were the prime caregivers during infancy !Kung children were surrounded by concerned adults and other children. For at least the first year infants were carried in a sling at the mother's side. This closeness enabled the infants to accommodate to the mothers' movements and the mothers to respond speedily to their needs. Feeding was almost continuous and the onus seemed to be on the infant to show satiation by dropping the nipple rather than to show hunger by crying. Weaning took place at two to three years but before this the infant would both feed and play with the mother's breast.

> Nursing often occurs simultaneously with active play with the free breast, languid extension-flexion movements in the arms and legs, mutual vocalization, face to face interaction (the breasts are quite long and flexible) and various forms of self touching, including occasional masturbation. (Devore and Konner, 1974, p. 130)

The infants moved away from the mother as soon as they became mobile but returned frequently. The mothers continued to carry the infants until the birth of the next child and this 'weaning from being carried' did result in some initial protest. However, the children soon turned to peers and within a year of ceasing to be carried social behaviour was centred on the peer group. The mothers therefore seemed close, nurturant and responsive to their infants for at least four or five years, with breastfeeding playing a crucial part in protecting the infant from infection. San fathers played with their infants but had a secondary role in comparison with the mothers. As Devore and Konner commented, 'their possibilities are limited by the fact that they have no breasts' (ibid p. 138).

A comparative study of infancy does show features which appear in both non-human primates and man. These features are probably phylogenetic adaptations and could therefore be expected to occur in contemporary families. Firstly, infants are dependent and mothers nurturant. Secondly, the pair are characterised by close physical proximity, certainly for the first few months and usually for several years. Thirdly, this prolonged period of dependent immaturity, in a safe environment, enables the infant to show curiosity, exploration and play, which requires separation from the mother. Fourthly, caregiving can be a function of other adults in the group but such multiple contacts are not always a feature of infant experience. When both human and non-human infants do have access to a wider group of adults and peers, as in the bonnet macaques and the !Kung San, their future behaviour, particularly concerning separation from the mother, differs from that of infants reared more exclusively by their mothers.

The role of the father

Having concentrated on the infant in a non-human and a human context it is now time to consider the second member of the family unit, namely the father. The degree to which the father shares in the care of his infant will be found to vary both between species and within species. In general, selective pressures ensure that any behaviour, for example paternal nuturance, which is characteristic of a particular species or group is likely to exist because such behaviour has facilitated the reproductive success of that species. Likewise if we find variations of behaviour within a species then it is probable that environmental variations have made certain behavioural patterns the most successful in that particular setting. Therefore variations in the amount of paternal caretaking are likely to be related to the extent to which such care is necessary for survival. Another factor to be taken into account when considering paternal care is whether females are biologically more predisposed to care for their infants, and are more nurturant than are males. There is some evidence from animal studies that this is the case. Pre-adolescent male monkeys reared in isolation were found to be both more aggressive and less nurturant when placed with infants than were females reared under the same conditions (Chamove, Harlow and Mitchell, 1967). Since both sexes had been reared in isolation no learning could have taken place; and since both groups were pre-pubescent significant sex-linked hormonal differences cannot have been responsible. However, it has been shown that if female mammals are given male sex hormone before they are born their behaviour as adults will be less nurturant towards infants than will that of normal females (Fuller, Zarrow, Anderson and Denenberg, 1970). In a human study it was found that ten-year-old girls who had a high level of androgen in their system shortly before birth were more 'tomboyish' and less interested in marriage and motherhood than were a matched group of girls who were non-androgenized (Money and Ehrhardt, 1972). Females may, therefore, be more predisposed to nurture infants than are males but since culture affects the biologically given we can expect considerable individual variation in both male and female behaviour as a result of ecological and psychological factors.

West and Konner (1976) considered father-infant relationships cross-phylogenetically by making use of the concept of 'parental' investment.

This concept was originally developed by Trivers (1972) and defined as 'any investment that enhances the offspring's chance of surviving at the cost of the parent's ability to invest in another offspring' (p. 139). It was found that the extent to which the male or the female takes part in rearing the young is part of a group of factors which includes mating and courtship behaviour, differences between the sexes in appearance, and the type of sexual competition for mates. In general, although many exceptions can occur, males will take less care of the young than females in a system in which (1) one male lives and mates with several females; (2) males compete with each other for the females; (3) males are slightly larger and, perhaps, more brightly coloured than females. At the other end of this continuum females will take less care of the young than males when one female lives and mates with several males, when the females compete for the males, and when the females are larger and more brightly coloured. The human species comes in the centre of this continuum (see Table 1.2).

Table 1.2 *Continuum of parental investment and related variables* (From West and Konner, 1976)

	Elephant seals, baboons, macaques	*Monogamous birds, man, marmosets*	*Polyandrous birds*
Parenting	Male parental investment lower than female parental	Male and female parental investment about equal	Female parental investment lower than male parental investment
Mating system	Polygyny	Monogamy	Polyandry
Courtship	Male-male competition for females, female choice	Low intrasex competition	Female-female competition for males, male choice
Adult sex differences	Males larger, higher metabolic rate, perhaps more brightly coloured, etc.	Low sexual dimorphism	Females larger etc.

Amongst mammals, as West and Konner point out, it is unusual to find males investing more than females except when ecological factors influence the male. Male investment is related to whether he lives with the mother and infant pair or alone. If he lives with the mother and infant, if resources are scarce and they need protection, then his level of investment will be higher than if resources are plentiful, predators scarce and he lives alone. In addition the more isolated the male and female pair the higher the level of male investment. An interesting human parallel to this was found by Bott over twenty years ago (Bott, 1955). She was concerned with the question of 'segregated' or 'joint' conjugal roles by which she meant the extent to which husband and wife spent their leisure time together, shared household duties – including caring for the children – and had friends in common. She found that there was considerable segregation of roles if the husband and wife lived in a close neighbourhood in which 'everybody knew everybody'. When the husband and wife were more isolated, and living in a neighbourhood where people were comparative strangers, both to the couple concerned and to each other, joint roles developed. Typically, segregated roles would occur if the husband and wife and the people they knew had grown up together and if they continued to live in the same neighbourhood after their marriage. Joint roles were more characteristic of couples who had moved to a new town or had each moved away from their own home towns before they met and married.

In non-human primates it is necessary to distinguish between paternal 'care' and paternal 'protection', a distinction which owes more to ecological setting than to phylogenetic differences. For example, amongst new world monkeys the males who will show most 'care' are those who live in isolated pairs or extended families and who are arboreal and omnivorous. Thus the marmoset male is wholly responsible for carrying and grooming the infant and assists in the birth (Snyder, 1972). The old world monkeys do not 'care' for their infants but will protect and defend them. These monkeys show characteristics associated with low male parental investment: polygyny, male-male competition, and males larger than females.

For the human male ecological setting is again important. West and Konner (1976) looked at fathering cross-culturally and concluded that paternal care would vary but within a range. In non-industrial societies fathers, typically, took a smaller part in infant care and child rearing than did the mothers. However three distinct patterns were observed: (1) If the society had accumulated resources the men would be primarily engaged in defending them. They would engage in warfare, marry several wives and take little part in child care. At times they were harsh and punitive and inspired fear in their children. (2) If the need for defence and warfare were reduced, and if the wife could make a reasonable contribution to the family resources, the father was likely to live with her and take more part in infant care. Husband and wife intimacy appeared to be greatest amongst cultures without accumulated resources or capital investment which needed to be defended (Whiting and Whiting, 1975). (3) If both the man's need to defend the accumulated resources and the need for the woman to provide resources were reduced, for example if more sophisticated methods of agriculture such as ploughing took the place of gathering, then monogamy would follow and the males' main contribution would be to provide resources. Thus if male parental investment is divided into 'defence', 'care' and 'provision of resources' then one or other will take precedence depending on the demands of the environment. In industrialised societies where the monogamous nuclear family is the norm and the defence of resources has been taken over by the state one could expect high paternal care except for the fact that provision of resources may require the male to spend considerable periods of time outside the home. This has the effect of reducing the quantity of time the father can be with his infant but need not affect the quality of the interaction.

The father's relationship with his infant is clearly less attached to biology than is the mother's. He has not felt the infant grow within him for several months. He has not given birth. He cannot breastfeed the infant nor has his body undergone the physical changes associated with pregnancy, birth and lactation. Nevertheless, studies of paternal response to birth (Bradley, 1963; Greenberg and Morris, 1974; Parke and O'Leary, 1975) showed that the fathers felt strongly attached to their infants and, in fact, interacted with them as much as their mothers. They found that when both parents were together with the infant the middle-class fathers held and rocked their babies more than the mothers; and working-class fathers held the infants more, looked at them more and gave them more physical auditory stimulation than did their wives.

As the infant grows older, if the father interacts with him, he is likely to direct almost the same amount of preferential smiling and looking towards the father as towards the mother. Surveys, however, of father-infant interaction suggest that fathers do not spend much time with their infants. Pedersen and Robson (1969) judged that the fathers in their sample played about eight hours per week with their nine-month-old infants, only 25 per cent of the fathers interviewed by Kotelchuck (1972) claimed to take any part in caring for their infants and the middle-class fathers studied by Ban and Lewis (1974) played with their one-year-olds for an average of fifteen minutes per day. Typically the father appears to play with the infant whilst the mother is responsible for caregiving. Thus during the early months, if this is the case, the father's role seems to be to support the mother and to interact with the infant sufficiently to be recognised. It is during the separation/individuation process, starting in the second half of the first year, that the father's role becomes particularly crucial for healthy infant development (see p. 91).

The role of the mother

To complete this description of the primary family unit the role of the mother must be explicated. Although this has been more extensively studied than that of the father it must not be automatically assumed that the infant is more affected by her than by the father. On the contrary, if the family unit is essentially interactive each participant will influence the others both directly and indirectly. Nevertheless, the dependent infant needs nurturance and, for both human and non-human infants, it is most usual for the mother to be the main source of such nurturance. Therefore her influence will be particularly strong during the early weeks when the infant is totally dependent and unable to distinguish clearly between himself and others. Since his early attempts at efficacy, or environmental manipulation, are likely to be directed towards the nurturing mother, although she is not recognised as such, her reaction to these attempts is of particular interest to anyone concerned with the development of the infant's belief in his own efficacy.

Mother-infant interaction has been shown (Sander, 1962) to have distinct characteristics which are specific to a certain stage in the infant's development. Sander called the first period that of 'initial adaption' and it was found to last from birth to approximately 2½ months. During this period the infant established a routine of sleeping and waking, feeding and eliminating, which made his behaviour more predictable for the mother. The mother in turn came to 'know' her baby and be able to respond appropriately to his cues. A synchrony developed between the infant's needs and the mother's care with special reference to his basic requirements to live and thrive. To achieve this the mother needed to combine empathy with objectivity; objectivity was important in enabling the mother to see the infant as an individual and not as a projection of her own wishes, needs, and anxieties. The second period from approximately 2½-5 months was known as that of 'reciprocal exchange' in which the mother, now less anxious about her adequacy in meeting her infant's basic needs, enjoyed interacting with him, particularly once smiling appeared. It was at this stage that mutual playful exchanges began to occur. The period 5-9 months showed the 'early directed activity of the infant', when the infant attempted to stimulate the mother to respond to him. The mother had to become sensitive to social and affective infant cues just as she had to learn to interpret his needs in the first period. Successful negotiation of these periods enabled the infant to progress to the two subsequent periods of 'focalization on mother' (9-15 months) and 'self assertion' (12-15 months) (see p. 90).

In order for the mother to respond to her infant's signals she needs, above all, to feel concern for his welfare. Winnicott (1958) described the mother's state as 'primary maternal preoccupation' which he called

> a very special psychiatric condition of the mother, of which I would say the following things: it gradually develops and becomes a state of heightened sensitivity during, and especially towards the end of pregnancy. It lasts for a few weeks after the birth of the child. It is not easily remembered by the mothers once they have recovered from it. I would go further and say that the memory mothers have of their state tends to become repressed. This organized state (that would be an illness were it not for the fact of the pregnancy) could be compared with a withdrawn state, or a dissociated state, or a fugue, or even with a disturbance at a deeper level such as a schizoid episode in which some aspect of the personality takes over temporarily. (p. 302)

Winnicott's evidence for this statement came both from observations made in his practice as a paediatrician and from the analysis of his patients. Confirmatory evidence can be obtained from experimental and observational studies. Hormonal changes during pregnancy may predispose the mother to respond differentially to her infant, as was found with non-human primates (see p. 4). Physically the infant is attractive to adults in that waving, unco-ordinated limbs give an appearance of helplessness and, as Tinbergen (1951) and Brooks and Hochberg (1960) found, facial features which are characteristic of infancy (for example, full cheeks, large forehead, and the position of the eyes) act as a positive stimulus to adults.

Klaus, Trause and Kennell (1975) filmed mothers during their first ten minutes of contact with their newborn babies and found that when the infants were nude the mothers began by touching the infants' extremities with their finger tips and progressed to stroking the whole of the infant with their palms, showing rising excitement in the process. The mothers also looked at their infants' faces and showed particular interest in the eyes. Some mothers used a high pitched voice when they spoke to their infants. The authors concluded that, 'for survival of the human infant, several powerful inducers of attachment must operate quickly to tie the mother to her infant' (p. 78). These observers also commented on the excitement that was present during the birth in both the mothers and the helpers, particularly when the baby was delivered at home. On this point Bentovim (1975) commented 'When Dr Klaus showed the film . . . of a birth in Santa Cruz, there was a moment of excitement in the group here. The boundaries between each of us seemed to dissolve with the shared feeling. The potential for ecstasy therefore seems to be universally present . . . ' (p. 82-3). MacFarlane (1977) also filmed deliveries, but his were in a British maternity hospital, and he too commented on 'the emotional complexity, richness and passion of what actually happens' (p. 53).

A mother's intense interest in her infant (a first-born son) can be seen in a transcript of a video tape of the minutes after birth given by MacFarlane.

'Oh, oh, oh, oh look at his little mouth oh, oh. It's lovely. Look at his little face. His little nails. Oh. His little squashed up nose like your nose (*to father*). He has red hair . . . Oh, his cheeks are coming rosy, Look at his little head. Look at his little mouth. He's gone to sleep. I wonder whether he was sucking his thumb inside. He knows his face, look (*baby touching his face with a hand*) Oh get off (*baby appears to swipe away father's touching fingers*) . . . Look at his hair. Oh look, it's all fair there. He is going a nice colour now, aren't you (*to baby*)? He's blowing bubbles. His little hands are all wrinkled – looks like he's done the washing up, doesn't he? . . . Open your eyes then (*to the baby*). . . . Can you open your eyes then? . . . Hello (*as baby opens his eyes for the first time*). Oh, he's going (*imitates baby blinking*) Hello (*laughs*). Oh, his eyes are all stuck, Hello . . . He's got your eyes (*to husband*). Look, you've got beautiful blue eyes (*to baby*). What are you looking at me like that for? (*to baby*) . . . Oh, he's got a beautiful face . . . ' (Adapted from MacFarlane, pp. 90-7)

Brazelton (1975) discussing human maternal behaviour after delivery made an interesting remark, which relates to Winnicott's (1958) idea of maternal 'illness', when he said that the therapists of mothers whose personalities had been assessed by weekly psychoanalytic interviews during pregnancy, predicted that all of the mothers 'were likely to be psychotic when they got their babies' (p. 81). This prediction was not confirmed and Brazelton commented that

When the prediction indeed turned out to be wrong, we had to reorganize our thinking about the anxiety that normally occurs in pregnancy. It is something like this: anxiety and disruption of old concepts, through dreams, become part of a normal process, a kind of unwiring of all the old connections to be ready for the new role. As I began to look at what happened to these women as they assumed their new roles it became apparent that the mother's prenatal anxiety helped her to shape herself in a very powerful way around the individuality of the particular baby she had. I began to see this anxiety as very constructive for the women in coping with their new roles. (p. 81)

It is possible that the psychosis predicted by the therapists could have appeared as 'primary maternal preoccupation', which would not have been seen as psychotic. We could further hypothesise that the 'healthy illness' described by Winnicott may also occur during pregnancy in the form of heightened anxiety. It appears that most human mothers and other adults are characterised by intense interest and pleasure in their newborn babies which may well have a survival value.

This relatively prolonged state of immaturity in the human young is made possible, in turn, by strongly developed 'parenting' behaviour in the adults, and the human *males'* prolonged interest in the young is unmatched in any other primate ... despite the trend toward theoretically lower reproductive capability, hominization has been highly successful with regard to reproductive success, mainly, one would surmise, because of the high interest human mothers and fathers maintain in their offspring. (Freedman, 1974 p. 23)

Mahler (1965a) made a similar point when she claimed that the mother's empathy is the human equivalent of the survival instincts apparent in other animals, since without external aid the human infant would not survive. 'During the post-natal period, the intrauterine, parasite-host relationship has to be replaced by the infant's being enveloped, as it were, in the extrauterine matrix of the mother's nursing care, a kind of social symbiosis' (p. 224).

One of the first observable behaviours of the human infant is crying, which seems to elicit caregiving responses in the parents, especially the mother. It appears that the infant's behaviour, despite initial individual differences, will be influenced by the behaviour of the caregiver. Sander (1969) showed that when infants who had been together in a nursery for their first ten days were then separated into two groups, one of which was looked after by nurse A and one by nurse B, those who were in the care of nurse B cried much less than they had in the nursery whereas those with nurse A showed only a slight decrease. Nurse A responded promptly to the infants' cries but nurse B showed more sensitivity to individual differences. Bell and Ainsworth (1972) looked at changes in the amount of crying over the first year. They found that, if the year was divided into quarters, although the mothers' responsiveness was fairly stable throughout the year, the infants' behaviour changed by the third quarter: that is, if the mother was unresponsive in the first and second quarters the infant cried more frequently in the third and fourth quarters. The mothers of the infants who cried most frequently became even less likely to respond towards the end of the first year. Infant crying was also assessed in terms of general maternal care and it was found that, in all quarters, there was a negative correlation between frequency of crying and 'appropriate' maternal care. However, when Clarke-Stewart (1973) looked at older infants, aged 11, 14, and 17 months, she found that while, generally, the most responsive mothers had the children who cried the least this effect was destroyed when the children were grouped by sex. She found then that the girls who cried least and the girls who cried most had mothers who were among the most responsive. Dunn (1975) considered those infants who cried most and those who cried least at 14 and 20 weeks and found that while there was a positive correlation between maternal responsiveness and a low level of crying, there was no such relationship between responsiveness and a high level of crying.

It is possible that prompt response is not, in itself, sufficient to soothe an infant: what the mother does is also important. Korner and Thoman (1970, 1972) used six different calming techniques, in random order, with forty newborn babies to assess which was the most effective method. The techniques were:

1 The infant was lifted and put to the shoulder with head supported and with the face just above shoulder level.
2 The infant was lifted horizontally and was cradled in the arms in the nursing position.
3 The infant was held close while he remained lying down. He was not moved in any way.
4 The infant, who had previously been placed in an infant seat, was raised 55 degrees to an upright position.
5 The infant, in the infant seat, was moved to and fro as if in a perambulator.

6 The infant, lying supine, was talked to in a high pitched female voice. The voice was used as a marker for observation after a preliminary study had shown that the voice had no greater effect than no stimulation at all. (ibid. 1972)

The results showed that the first, shoulder position, was by far the most effective and that, in addition, this caused the infant to open its eyes and become visually alert. The next most successful method was raising the infant seat and it is possible that 'non-cuddlers', i.e. infants who resist close physical contact with their mothers, would prefer this (see page 27). It is interesting to note that when the mother holds her infant upright its position closely resembles that of the !Kung San infant in a sling on its mothers's side.

Some of the most subtle studies of interaction have been those concerned with adult-infant synchrony when the mother, or other adult, is stimulating rather than soothing the infant, although the two cannot always be separated since soothing enables the infant to be alert to the environment and receive a tolerable amount of stimulation from it. Much of the infant's early learning is dependent upon the mother since, 'mothers stimulate intensively, reinforce efficiently, and allow themselves to be manipulated; this informs children about the consequences of their own activity at a very early age' (Papoušek and Papoušek, 1975, p. 256). When stimulating, the mother needs to select a wide range of stimuli for her infant and to see that he receives them at a tolerable level. How she does this has been of considerable interest to researchers. Thoman et al. (1970, 1971, 1972) found, through filming mothers and their newborn infants, that mothers with their first babies (primiparous) took longer to feed them, altered their manner of feeding more often, and stimulated the baby more than did mothers who had given birth before (multiparous). The infants of these primiparous mothers sucked less and took in less food than did those of multiparous mothers, even though there was no difference between the groups when they were fed by a nurse. These studies exemplify the reciprocal influence of mother and infant. Indeed the outstanding characteristic of mother-infant interaction, and hence stimulation, is its mutuality.

Often the infant, unintentionally, initiates an activity by his spontaneous behaviour. The mother then joins in and paces her reaction by his. Collis and Schaffer (1975) studied the mutuality of infant-mother gaze which occurs when mother and infant both look at the same object. They found that the mother tended to look where the infant looked, and was thus able to comment on what he saw. She could also predict the infant's next move and therefore move an attractive object so that it was within his reach. Usually the mother's behaviour synchronised with the infant's. Brazelton, Koslowski and Main (1974) filmed mother-infant interaction sequences at weekly intervals starting when the infants were 4 weeks and ending when they were 20 weeks. They found that, as early as 4 weeks, the infant's behaviour towards his mother differed from his behaviour towards an object (in this study a furry toy monkey 3½ inches high). The authors commented that, 'by 4 weeks we could predict correctly from watching parts of his body and observing his span and degree of attention whether he was responding to the object or to his mother' (p. 55). When the object was presented the infant would stare at it with rapt attention which was interspersed with short bursts of jerky, agitated movements directed towards the object. As the object came closer he would look as if he was going to mouth it, or make swipes in its direction. He would then become inactive and look away from the object. When the infant was interacting with his mother the whole action was smoother. He would look at her, perhaps stretch out his limbs towards her, vocalise or grimace and then look away. The period of excited, intense interaction would end more gradually than it did with the object. The infant also tended to pace his interaction in response to his mother's and she was seen to do the same. Indeed, a mother's behaviour with her infant is unlike her behaviour with adults and seems peculiarly adapted to the infant's signals.

Stern (1974) filmed mothers and their infants in their own homes during play and feeding. He found that when the mothers interacted with their infants their speech was higher in pitch than usual and they tended to draw out their vowel sounds. Similarly their facial expressions were exaggerated. Expressions, such as surprise, were built up slowly and held for much longer than they would have been if the interaction had been with an adult. It would seem that the mother's behaviour is related to the infant's perceptual capabilities in that swifter and more subtle changes of expression could be confusing for the infant. Stern (1974) also studied mutual gaze, or eye contact, arguing that, as the visual motor system matures earlier than other forms of motor behaviour, by the time the infant is 3 months old both mother and infant will have the same amount of control over their visual behaviour. Eye contact was maintained for much longer between mother and infant – often over 30 seconds – than occurs between adults unless they are lovers or about to fight. If the infant caught the mother's eye and looked at her she was unlikely to turn away, similarly the infant was most likely to be stimulated to look at the mother when she both looked at and spoke to him and he too was less likely to look away when she was still in eye contact with him. The behaviour, then, of both mother and infant makes mutual gaze likely. It has been found (Kendon, 1967) that with adults the listener gazes at the speaker whereas the speaker looks initially at the listener and then periodically until the end of the utterance, when he will look back to signal that he is about to stop speaking and that the roles may be reversed. With mothers and infants the mother gazed at the infant as if he were talking whereas, in fact, she spoke for both of them. During the interaction the infant was likely to alternate between looking at and looking away from the mother, but she had continual gaze. It was found that in 94 per cent of all mutual gazes it was the infant who initiated and terminated the interaction.

There are times, however, when such reciprocal responsiveness is absent and we get what Stern (1977) called 'mis-steps in the dance'. Sometimes the mother will be overstimulating and the infant will attempt to avoid her gaze by moving his head away. If the mother does not interpret this signal correctly she will increase her efforts, rather than lowering the level of stimulation; the interaction then becomes intolerable for the infant and frustrating for the mother. The obverse of this is the mother who understimulates her infant either because she does not react to his initiatory activities or because she terminates the interaction too soon by stopping when the infant looks away, not realising that infants have a pattern of looking away followed by looking back. Sometimes the infant's behaviour does not stimulate the mother sufficiently to make her respond, or she is required to make much greater efforts than is usual. Stern gave details of a particularly unsatisfactory relationship between a mother and one of her twin sons called Fred. Their interaction had a characteristic pattern: it would start with a mutual gaze but, when his mother moved towards him, Fred would look away. The mother would not interpret this as a sign for her to stop moving or to draw back but, on the contrary, she would move closer. Fred would then move further away and move his head to one side. He would then turn back towards her, whereupon she would start withdrawing and the sequence would be repeated in reverse with her withdrawing and Fred following. She would then look elsewhere but Fred would continue to monitor her movements and make small shadowing movements even though her attention was no longer on him. She, however, would notice these movements and turn back towards him which would result in his withdrawing and the whole unhappy sequence would restart. Their behaviour made it appear that they were unable to get together and unable to remain apart. (Stern commented that, in his second year, Fred was less attached to his mother than was his twin but he also had more difficulties in separating from her in that he would return to her frequently rather than remain on his own to play.)

Throughout such interactive episodes the infant has to learn to adapt his responses to those of his mother but, it is argued, he also learns, when interaction is synchronised that his behaviour can affect his mother. On the other hand, if his attempts to initiate interaction are ignored or if the interaction is discordant it is believed that the infant will not develop the notion that his environment is ordered and able to be affected by him, since the important conceptual link between his behaviour and the behaviour of others will not have been made. If this early experience of mutuality is lacking the infant's development will be affected, not because of some traumatic happening, but because he has not been able to build up a realistic picture of the world and his place in it. Rather he is left realising that things happen to him, but not *why* they happen nor that he can play his part in their occurrence. Winnicott (1952) strongly supported this line of reasoning:

> The basis for mental health is being laid down by the mother from conception onwards through the ordinary care that she gives her infant because of her special orientation to that task. Mental ill health of psychotic quality arises out of delays and distortions, regressions and muddles in the early stages of growth . . . (p.227-8)

Mahler (1965a) did not wholly agree with Winnicott's views since she claimed that in her practice she had seen psychotic infants whose mothers would have been described by Winnicott as 'ordinary devoted mothers'. Her comment on these infants was that, 'We could reconstruct in some cases such extreme, seemingly intrinsic vulnerability on the part of the child which even the most favourable environmental situations could not conceivably have counteracted, thus preventing infantile psychosis' (p. 225).

The belief that the infant learns that he can be effective through his mother's response to him needs to be carefully interpreted. The notion that a precondition for subsequent faulty adaptation is a particular type of maladaptive handling in infancy, with the converse that 'good enough mothering' (Winnicott, 1958) will lead to healthily adaptive emotional growth, could imply that we are using the simple language of cause and effect. Thus if a person has a cut hand we assume that, prior to the appearance of the wound, an actual 'cutting event' occurred. By analogy it could be argued that if a child, or an adult, shows emotional disturbance there has been a prior 'disturbing event'. There are, however, difficulties with this analogy in that disturbed behaviour is more likely to arise from the person's appraisal of the *current* situation than to be related to a single 'disturbing event' in the past. The past, however, may effect his appraisal of the current situation and hence his response to it. Jahoda (1977) reminds us of St Augustine's conception of time which encompassed a 'threefold present': 'a present of things past but remembered now, a present of things present and experienced now, a present of things future but anticipated now' (p. 62). Therefore when discussing the significance of experiences in infancy, rather than thinking in terms of cause and effect, we should consider how the infant's belief in his own efficacy and his place in the world develops through these experiences, since it will be this belief which will, in the future, affect his appraisal of a current situation – which will, in turn, affect his subsequent behaviour.

Observational studies of mother-infant interaction do point to the reciprocal influence of mother and infant. The infant's first impression of the animate and inanimate environment will, in the absence of any other evidence, be formed by her behaviour unless, and until, his first impressions are disconfirmed by subsequent interactions. However, the perception of future events may be influenced by the expectations the infant or child has developed previously. How, then, are these initial impressions formed? Let us assume that at birth the infant experiences, for example, hunger, tiredness, and pain and is able to react to these sensations with cries or bodily movements which will differ in intensity from infant to infant (see p. 25). The hungry infant will cry and he will associate the feeling of tension caused by hunger with, firstly, reacting by crying and secondly, if his cry has been previously answered by feeding, with the reaction of nutritive sucking. However, there is a difference between these two reactions in that the crying reaction is under his control, that is, it occurs whenever he needs to cry, but a delay will be experienced between the wish to suck nutritively and the appearance of the relevant object, i.e. a breast or a bottle. Initially the infant could not be expected to be able to distinguish between the act of crying, which is under his control, and the object for nutritive sucking, which is under someone else's control. However, after the first few feeds, it is possible that the infant has developed the ability to 'know what he wants': the feeling of a breast or bottle in his mouth on which he can suck. If his wish is closely followed by the appearance of the actual object required he will build up, by association, an expectation that needs are met. This is an important development both emotionally and cognitively since it leads to the feeling that the environment has consistency. However, if the appearance of the breast or bottle is not related to his feeling of need, either because his crying is ignored or because he is fed on a schedule which may involve waking him to feed him, then either he adapts and learns to respond to stimuli which impinge on him, i.e. to feed when the bottle or breast appears – or he remains in confusion with no means of relating to an environment which appears to be entirely unpredictable. In the normal course of events the infant's needs and signals will not always meet with an immediate response. However, once he has built up the expectation that there will be a response to him he will become able to wait for a short time, perhaps soothing himself by finger sucking; this ability to wait is a sign that the first developmental period has been negotiated satisfactorily. At this stage it is unlikely that the infant is aware that his needs are met by someone outside himself, or that the consistent or inconsistent environment is external. To make this distinction will be the achievement of the next stage of development.

2
The origins of competence

Introduction

From the moment of birth the infant is thinking, feeling, perceiving and physically active. While it is true that one motive for his behaviour is his desire to have physical needs such as hunger and thirst satisfied, White (1960) suggested that the infant is also motivated by a desire to have an effect upon his environment and that it is this 'effectance motivation' which causes him to actively explore his environment and to manipulate the objects and people within it. When the infant explores or manipulates objects and people he is not attempting to assuage some physiological need but rather he is learning about the environment at moments when he is in comparative safety and physically comfortable.

> Effectance is to be conceived as a neurogenic motive, in contrast to a viscerogenic one. It can be informally described as what the sensori-neuro-muscular system wants to do when it is not occupied with homeostatic business. Its adaptive significance lies in its promotion of spare-time behaviour that leads to an extensive growth of competence, well beyond what could be learned in connection with drive reduction. (p. 147)

Such learning may of course be useful in the future when the infant needs to seek shelter from danger or satisfy physiological needs. White argued that competence could be manifested in the infant and child's interactions with both people and things and should not be seen as a discrete aspect of his personality. It develops because of the intrinsic reward obtained when mastery or success is obtained in any particular activity. An illustration, given by White, of the infant's intrinsic wish to be effective is that of the one-year-old who wishes to feed himself rather than be fed by his mother.

Were he only motivated by a desire for food he would let his mother feed him as he would obtain more food in this way. However the infant seems to prefer the autonomous activity of feeding himself more than the sheer taking in of food. Connolly and Bruner (1974) believed that

> 'competence implies action, changing the environment as well as adapting to the environment. It seems in a sense to involve at least three things. First, being able to select features from the total environment that provide the relevant information for elaborating a course of action. . . . Secondly, having planned a course of action, the next task is to initiate the sequence of movements or activities, in order to achieve the objective we have set ourselves. And finally, we must utilize what we have learnt from our successes and failures in the formulation of new plans. (p. 3)

As the infant achieves what he sets out to do so he will develop that subjective sense of competence which we are concerned with here. In particular he will develop a sense of competence with reference to his ability to meet the challenges posed by new cognitive tasks both at home and, especially, at school. In this chapter we will consider the infant's cognitive and communicative abilities as well as individual differences in temperament and motivation, since the latter will affect both the quality of his effectance motivation and others' response to his early strivings, while the former are prerequisites for his being able to attempt to manipulate the environment.

Individual differences at birth

It appears that mothers are predisposed to nurture their dependent infants. Nevertheless the infant's ability to facilitate or inhibit such maternal responsiveness must be taken into account. Infants have been found to differ at birth, both physically and temperamentally, and such individual differences could be expected to affect the conscious and unconscious behaviour of the parents. For example, in his study of battered children Gill (1970) pointed out that parents often battered only one child in the family and that these same children attracted abuse in their subsequent foster homes even though no other children had been so treated in those homes. He concluded that the child's behaviour was as important in cases of 'battering' as was the deviance of the parents or a stressful environment. It seems that a significant factor in the development of satisfactory interaction between parent and infant is the extent to which an infant's particular characteristics are acceptable to the parents.

One difference often observed between infants at birth is their activity level. An early series of studies of this were Fries's investigations of neonates' (newborns') sensori-motor response to stimuli. Fries, writing in 1971, referred to her earlier work in which she had argued that

> ... it seemed reasonable to conjecture that the neonates' response was due to a combination of genetic endowment, intrauterine experiences, and the birth process. The term *core* was used to encompass the reactive mechanism resulting from the interaction of these three elements. We called the core's sensori-motor response the *congenital activity type*. (p. 275)

She then tested the neonates' responses to having a padded weight dropped near them and having the breast or bottle, which they were sucking, removed for one minute. She was able to divide the infants into three 'normal' groups, the 'active', the 'moderately active' and the 'quiet' with two extreme, possibly pathological, groups at either end – the 'hyperactive' and the 'hypoactive'. She further claimed that by six weeks there was some modification of the initial congenital activity type due to the mother's reaction with a critical period for change between 3 and 4 weeks. Birns (1965) added to her findings by showing that within the first five days of life individual differences could be found in infants' strength of reaction to external stimuli (in Birns's study the external stimuli were a soft tone, a loud tone, a cold disc placed on the infant's thigh and a dummy put in the mouth). The infants observed consistently showed a strong, a moderate, or a mild response to the stimuli, regardless of its type.

Cytryn (1968) remarked that Fries's global description of activity needed to be broken down into more discrete categories and, indeed, this has now been done. For example Escalona (1968) made a distinction between 'active' and 'inactive' infants. Between 4 and 12 weeks the inactive infants showed a greater tendency to suck when they were not feeding, could focus their eyes and gazed at objects around them and explored their environment by touching it. The active infants made more gross bodily movements and responded to a lower level of stimulation than the inactive. The inactive however could soothe themselves by their self-initiated sucking. In terms of the environment the active seemed less dependent on it for stimulation whereas the inactive were less dependent on it for comfort. Escalona suggested that the calmness of the inactive infants could result in adults failing to give them the stimulation they needed. An alternative view (Murphy and Moriarty, 1976) is that in the early weeks the inactive baby will be less affected by disturbing stimuli, although he will also be less able to discharge tension by gross motor activity.

In addition to activity level infants have been found to vary in other ways in their responsiveness to stimuli. Escalona (1968) showed considerable individual differences in the infant's autonomic responses, i.e. changes in heart rate or respiratory rate. Korner (1964), in a study of response to auditory stimuli, demonstrated that some infants gave a whole body undifferentiated response, others gave a single response and others showed several reactions which could, however, be differentiated. She also found that when infants were given a dummy and then had a light shone into their eyes, as part of an opthalmological examination, some of them would respond by sucking more strongly whereas others would stop completely. She and Grobstein (1967) argued that the individual differences found among infants in their readiness to respond to visual, auditory, textural and tactile stimuli indicated variations in their ability to withstand the demands of internal stimuli and their degrees of need for a stimulus barrier to filter out external stimuli. The question of the infants' ability to control incoming stimuli was taken up by Murphy and Moriarty (1976) who found that some infants were more successful than others at shutting out anything which was too intense for them. They commented that the infants' success was, to an extent, dependent on their individual areas of sensitivity; for example, infants who wished to avoid a too intense visual stimulus could shut their eyes, whereas it was more difficult for them to shut their ears to an unduly loud sound.

Another area in which individual variation is found is in the infant arousal level known as its 'state'. That is, the infant can be deeply asleep with little or no movement; half-asleep with some movement and, perhaps, whimpering; awake and alert with eyes open; awake and crying. The awake and alert state appears to be of particular value to adults who can engage in eye contact with the infant at this time and who can bring it about by stimulating or calming the infant (Bennett, 1971). It is also in this state that the infants are most able to make use of external stimuli. Considerable variation has been found between infants in the length of time they spend in this awake and alert state. It is possible that variations in infant behaviour with respect to state may have a predictive function since Heider (1966) found that when they were of school age children who, as infants, were active when awake but very still when asleep differed from those children who, as infants, had shown movement or restlessness in their sleep. Some infants are more able than others to convey their state, for example, the fact that they are hungry or tired. Korner and Grobstein (1967) pointed out that their competence in this will affect the mother's self-confidence by making her feel secure in her ability to interpret her infant's state. They also say that some infants may not *experience* their states very distinctly, which 'may delay the formation of internal sets of expectations and the discrimination between external and internal reality, possibly predisposing to later regression in this discrimination' (p. 70). It is possible that if the mother, or caregiver, misinterprets the infant's state and, for example, insists of feeding when the infant is not hungry then the infant will become confused (see p. 22).

Korner (1964) found that infants also differed in their 'zone reliance' (for example, the incidence of oral, mouthing activities in contrast to erections or startles) as well as in 'mode reliance' (i.e. the way they used their mouths, showing variation in being primarily interested in sucking, chewing, spitting, biting or drooling). Some infants were found to tolerate the effect of hunger for longer than others before it resulted in regression — i.e. a breakdown in hand-mouth coordination.

A particularly interesting study of individual differences in neonates was that of Schaffer and Emerson (1964b), who found that infants differed in the extent to which they enjoyed being 'cuddled'. Both the 'cuddlers' and the 'non-cuddlers' sought comfort from their mothers, but the first group accepted close physical contact, were more placid, slept more and took more interest in cuddly toys; the second group resisted being cuddled and were more restless, being particularly resistant to being dressed or tucked into bed. This difference was found to be independent of the mother's behaviour. Obviously considerable difficulties could be caused by a mother who continued to cuddle a resisting infant. Schaffer and Emerson found that the mothers of the non-cuddlers had to comfort them by distracting them in a way which was acceptable to the infant rather than in the way which seemed 'natural' to them as mothers. Thoman (1975) gives a detailed account of the early months of a 'rejecting' infant who did not like to be held. In this study the observers noted that the infant, although being alert and awake in the cot, became drowsy and cried when picked up. The mother did not appear to notice this consciously, but the amount of time she spent looking at his face when feeding him dropped from 16 per cent at 10 days to 8 per cent at six weeks. At six weeks the observers pointed out the details of the infant's behaviour to the parents and suggested that they should use the cradle board as much as possible so that the infant could see what was going on without being held. At four months the infant seemed to be developing normally and the mother had adapted to his behaviour, even to the extent of carrying him with his back towards her so that he faced away from her.

The infant's sex may affect the way in which the mother responds. Moss (1967) found that there were clear differences related to sex in mothers' handling of their infants at three weeks and these were still apparent, but less striking at three months. At three weeks the mothers held the male infants about 27 minutes more per 8 hours than they did the females and at three months about 14 minutes more. The females slept more than the males and were less irritable. The mothers tended to respond less to the more frequent cries of the boys but to respond more often when the girls cried. The girls, in turn, were more likely to respond to their mothers' soothing. When interacting with their infants the mothers stimulated and aroused the boys whereas they tended to repeat, or imitate, the vocalisations of the girls.

Sander (1969) also found that, at as early as ten days, the girls slept more and that differences in treatment, in the first ten days, affected boys and girls differentially. Girls who had been cared for in a nursery for the first ten days and then moved to the care of a single surrogate mother showed a considerable spurt in developing a pattern of sleeping at night and being alert in the day, whereas girls who had had a single surrogate all along developed more gradually. The boys advanced rapidly in the days 11-29 if they had received surrogate mothering throughout and were retarded by the nursery experience.

During the first few months initial differences can cohere so that the infants display different 'personalities'. These are often observed by their caregivers in the early days of life and may well become self-fulfilling prophecies. Bennett (1971) gave personality sketches of three infants in a nursery and observed the effect of the infants on their caregiver both in terms of their assessment of the infants and their response to them.

Smith Baby boy Smith was a sturdy and handsome infant. At the age of 3 days he showed characteristics which he maintained throughout: long periods of alertness without much fussing, and easy arousal, awakening without a cry and easy calming. These characteristics were viewed as indications of a basic good nature, and a solid and happy temperament . . . The amount of care he received was considerable for a busy nursery. He would be carried round while simple chores were performed and during discussions and shift changes would usually be held on someone's lap.

Brown Baby girl Brown had a round face with fat cheeks and strikingly rich curly black hair . . . Brown had the ability to sustain alertness for long periods. Her activity level was below average. In the main she cried with hunger but she was easily pacified. During most of the morning a glance in her direction would encounter her profuse hair, her wide full eyes, and her motionless body . . . The staff viewed this as evidence of a calm and even temper, as well as niceness and femininity. There were cries, but they were not urgent except with hunger; and this was interpreted as modesty and consideration . . . The personality that emerged was that of a simple feminine girl who was not sexy or flirtatious . . . The amount of handling she received was average. She was hugged and cuddled at times of bathing, feeding, and changing, and variably at other times depending on who felt she was cute. This child had an early capacity for visual engagement, but did not receive much face-to-face contact.

Jones Baby boy Jones . . . was lean and well-built. At 5 days it was noted that he was easy to awaken but would not remain alert unless jiggled and rocked . . . at 15 days, the child displayed a general irritability. Crying was frequent. He was unable to maintain alertness without intervention. After a half minute of activity with limb thrashing, the trunk would stiffen and he would begin to cry unless some sort of pacification was initiated. The amount of rocking required was small and for the most part if he was merely held he remained calm. A type of body movement that most observers found to be unpleasant was a sudden stiffening of his trunk; this was often interpreted as a rejection . . . A staff attitude appeared during the second week which became outspoken at 15 days. It amounted to: this is a disagreeable child. 'He's irritable and tightens up and gets purple so he doesn't get held as much.' At 18 days . . . though he was seen as pained and unhappy, he alienated himself from sympathy by what was interpreted as his attitude of open rejection and disagreeableness. By his greed, defiance and unreasonable rages he made himself an outcast. (pp. 81-5)

These sketches show the extent to which the infant's initial behaviour and appearance can affect the care he receives which will, in turn, affect his subsequent behaviour. Freud (1937) maintained that 'each individual ego is endowed from the beginning with its own peculiar dispositions and tendencies'; and Chess (1970) makes a similar point when she says:

The term temperament . . . refers to the behavioral style of an individual child – the *how* (manner) of his behaviour rather than the *what* (content) or *why* (motivation). Each child has a characteristic way of reacting to new persons or situations, for example. Each has a typical level of energy expenditure or an individual threshold of response to sensory stimuli. (p. 122)

Chess and her colleagues (Thomas, Chess and Birch, 1968) conducted a logitudinal study of 136 children from middle-class families and found that the children could be divided into 'easy' children, 'difficult' children, and 'slow to warm up' children in terms of clusters of temperamental traits. A most significant finding was that, initially, the children's traits seemed to be independent of parental characteristics, but parental reactions to these traits did subsequently affect development. During their study they were able to distinguish nine discrete categories of behaviour which together composed the individual child's temperament:

1 *Activity level* (Motor component of child's functioning. Proportion of active to inactive periods.)
2 *Rhymicity* (Regularity and predictability of for example hunger, feeding pattern, elimination and sleep-wake cycle.)
3 *Approach or withdrawal* (Tendency to move towards or away from unfamiliar people, objects, or situations.)
4 *Adaptability* (Speed and ease with which current behaviour can be modified in response to altered environmental structuring.)
5 *Quality of mood* (Amount of pleasant, joyful or friendly behaviour and unpleasant, unfriendly behaviour or crying.)
6 *Intensity of reaction* (Energy level of response irrespective of its quality or direction.)
7 *Threshold of responsiveness* (Intensity level of stimulation required to evoke a discernable response to sensory stimuli, environmental objects and social contacts.)
8 *Distractibility* (The effectiveness of extraneous environmental stimuli in interfering with or in altering the direction of ongoing behaviour.)
9 *Attention span and persistence* (The length of time an activity is pursued and its continuation in the face of obstacles to maintaining the activity direction.)

Many of these categories are similar to the individual differences found to be present in the first few days of life, and therefore the question of the consistency of these differences is crucial. As early as 1937 Gessell and Ames had distinguished fifteen traits:

1 *Energy output* (General amount and intensity of activity.)

2 *Motor demeanor* (Postural bearing, general muscular control and poise, motor coordination and facility of motor adjustment.)

3 *Self-dependence* (General self-reliance and self-sufficiency without appeal to the assistance of others.)

4 *Social responsiveness* (Positive reactivity to persons and to the attitudes of adults and of other children.)

5 *Family attachment* (Closeness of affection: degree of identification in the family group.)

6 *Communicativeness* (Expressive reference to others by means of gesture and vocalization.)

7 *Adaptivity* (General capacity to adjust to new situations.)

8 *Exploitation of environment* (Utilisation and elaboration of environment and circumstances in order to gain new experience.)

9 *'Humor' sense* (Sensitiveness and playful reactiveness to surprise, novelty and incongruity in social situations.)

10 *Emotional maladjustment* (Balance and stability of emotional response in provocative situations.)

11 *Emotional expressiveness* (Liveliness and subtlety of expressive behavior in emotional situations.)

12 *Reaction to success* (Expression of satisfaction in successful endeavor.)

13 *Reaction to restriction* (Expressiveness of behavior in reaction to failure, discomfort, disappointment, frustration.)

14 *Readiness of smiling* (Facility and frequency of smiling.)

15 *Readiness of crying* (Promptness and facility of frowning and tears.)

On these traits they assessed five infants at the age of one year, and then considered whether the same traits would be found with the same intensity when the children were five. The answer was positive and, in addition, they found that for three of the infants the following traits and their intensity were noted before sixteen weeks: energy output, motor demeanor, self-dependence, emotional expressiveness, and readiness of smiling. The traits of social responsiveness, communicativeness and adaptivity were also noticeable in two of the children. Macfarlane (1964) however concluded, after a growth study lasting thirty-five years, that change was more noticeable than continuity in the behaviour of her subjects. It is unlikely that a simple one-to-one correspondence will be found between individual differences at birth and individual differences later in life, but it would be surprising if no continuity were found and, indeed, some of the studies quoted – Escalona, 1968; Fries and Wolf, 1971; Korner and Grobstein, 1967; Murphy and Moriarty, 1976; Thomas, Chess and Birch, 1968 – do point to continuity. Korner's (1971) threefold classification of the effect of early individual differences is useful in judging their significance. She argued that these differences may only be observable, in their pure form, for a short time, after which they will become part of the content of the developmental process; but that they may affect the way in which the infant approaches and masters the various developmental tasks, and that these differences will affect the infant's subjective experience of childhood events.

Yarrow (1964) made a similar point when he referred to 'dynamic continuity' in the personality, by which he meant that changes in observable behaviour are the result of developmental changes which are 'dynamically related' to earlier personality patterns. Some personality characteristics – for example, level of energy, expenditure of motivation to explore – were found to be consistent. Yarrow's main conclusions were that consistency was related to a consistent environment, and especially to an environment which reinforced existing characteristics. Characteristics were not found to be so consistent between chronologically adjacent development periods, e.g. infancy and pre-school, as they were between development periods which were *psychologically* similar. The child who was particularly negative as a two-year-old was more likely to show extremes of behaviour in adolescence than was one who was more amenable at that age. The argument being that, psychologically the third year of life and adolescence presented the child with similar challenges related to autonomy and identity formation.

Cognitive development

In the natural world the first sign of dawn is not the rising sun but rather the gradual diminution of darkness. Objects begin to appear as distinct shapes where previously only a deeper patch of blackness could be discerned. The undifferentiated becomes differentiated as the sky lightens: initial unity becomes duality and then plurality. In this manner, too, does the infant begin to comprehend his world cognitively. This process of comprehension requires the interaction of several fundamental systems – moving, sensing, feeling and thinking. Thus biological potential is actualised by the interaction of the motivated, maturing infant and a facilitating environment. The developmental task peculiar to this stage is one of differentiating both subjective activities and objective reality through infant-environment interaction. As the first two years pass the differentiated parts can begin to be named: language will develop and infancy will end.

The earliest and perhaps the most extensive description of infant cognitive development is that given by Piaget (1951, 1952, 1954) under the name 'sensori-motor intelligence'. Piaget's empirical data for infant development during the 'sensori-motor period', which covered the first two years was drawn almost entirely from observing the behaviour of his own three children. He divided this two-year period into six stages:

Stage 1 (0-1 month): At this time the infant merely uses the reflexes he is born with, but its significance is that the infant is starting to perform physical actions and, it is argued, through the repetition of these initially random and reflex actions, intelligence will develop. Piaget maintained that the infant will seek to repeat an action if that action has been profitable. For example, the infant initially puts his hand in or near his mouth and starts to suck it because of the sucking reflex. He will then repeat this action, making it more precise and refined by practice, until he can suck his thumb or his fingers. Thus the initial reflex action of sucking will develop, within the first year, into a co-ordinated series of actions which will enable the infant to suck his fingers, a toy or his blanket. Piaget believed that it was the initial chance action which causes the infant to repeat it, not an internal need, for example, to suck, which causes the initial action.

Stage 2 (1-4 months): This is the stage in which the infant starts to co-ordinate the reflex actions of the first month into what Piaget called 'primary circular reactions', by which he meant the end result of repeated action sequences which have, through continuous repetition, been refined and synchronised into a smooth sequence or habit. Thus hand moving and sucking can be put together to form thumb sucking. At this time the infant will repeat actions, such as grasping something he sees or looking at something that, while thrashing about, he has grasped, but is, as yet, incapable of intention. That is, he cannot think what he will do and then do it. All he can do at this stage is repeat and refine his action sequences.

Stage 3 (4-8 months): Now the infant will repeat actions in order to 'make interesting sights last' (Piaget, 1954). For example, if he has noticed that a toy hanging in his cot moves when he kicks it then he will go on kicking the toy to see it move again. Intentionality has started to appear and Piaget called these actions sequences 'secondary circular reactions'. However, at this age the infant's powers of thought are rudimentary and he will overgeneralise what he has observed. Thus if he has succeeded in making his toy move by kicking it he will also seek to make a bell ring again by kicking, apparently believing that the one action of toy kicking is sufficient to bring about a repetition of all the sights and sounds he wants to see and hear again. Although he has realised that actions have effects he has not sorted out the relationship between a particular action and its particular effect.

Stage 4 (8-12 months): These months show rapid development in that the infant's use of action becomes less magical and starts to take account of the real world; action and effect become co-ordinated. His behaviour begins to show both intention and purpose in that he is now able to set himself a goal (finding a toy) and will be able to keep this goal in mind whilst looking for the toy under a chair or a cushion without being distracted by the intervening action of looking under the chair or lifting the cushion. The ability to keep a goal in mind is clearly a sign of considerable cognitive sophistication since the infant must now be able to maintain an internal representation of a desired state (finding the toy) whilst carrying out a series of entirely different actions in the environment (seeking the toy). In addition, in order to seek a hidden toy the infant has to have learnt that an object continues to exist when he cannot see it and that the object that disappeared is the same object when he finds it. Piaget had argued that the infant originally acted as if his belief was that when he could not see an object it had ceased to exist and hence did not search for it. Piaget's views on the development of an understanding of object permanence have stimulated a considerable amount of subsequent experimental work (see p. 78). Although there is more involved in cognitive development than object permanence, nevertheless it is crucial for the infant to understand the properties of objects, and particularly the properties of animate objects, i.e. the significant people in his social environment. Piaget, however, concentrated on the infant's understanding of inanimate objects and also showed that at this stage the infant becomes able to use an object to enable him to obtain a goal which would, without the use of the intervening object, be unobtainable. For example, if a toy is out of reach on the other side of the table he now becomes capable of pulling the table cloth until the object comes within reach. He has thus begun to be a 'tool user', being able to understand that objects can have more than one function and can be adapted to serve his needs.

Stage 5 (12-18 months): Now curiosity and exploration, the 'tertiary circular reactions' appear. The infant no longer simply repeats actions or uses already perfected schemes, rather he actively looks for new properties in objects and tries out new forms of behaviour by experiment. It is an age in which the infant seems to seek novelty for its own sake and shows exhilaration in his accomplishments.

Stage 6 (18-24 months): In this final stage the toddler is still concerned with new ways of doing things but now he is less likely to experiment directly in the environment and more likely to think before he acts. His actions have begun to be internalised; a developmental process which, when completed, will give rise to the period of 'concrete operations' which starts about the age of seven. At two the toddler is beginning to be able to 'run through' an action sequence in his mind before trying it out in the real world. He is also showing signs of thinking of ways of doing something without actually trying each one. In a rudimentary way the two-year-old is able to use images, an aspect of his growing symbolic power. With the ability to use images, to internally represent and co-ordinate action schemes and, finally, to use verbal language, the period of sensori-motor intelligence and infancy comes to an end.

Recent studies of infant cognition have extended Piaget's original observations and theorising, and our understanding of the characteristics of sensori-motor intelligence. Bruner (1968, 1977), like Piaget, believes that cognition begins with physical action: 'As with so much early development, processes that later become internal – intention, attention, etc. – have an initial external motoric being that later goes underground' (1968, p. 579).

His studies of infant action, however, have considered behaviours quite different from the Piagetian circular reactions since he sees intellectual growth as dependent on the infant's *acting upon* the environment, not just upon understanding its properties through action. Thus, it is 'through development of successive hypotheses about the world and how our actions affect it the child climbs stepwise up the ladder of competence' (1977, p. 271). For example, he considered (1968) the way an infant uses his two hands and found that it was not until the end of the first year that the infant was able to hold an object in one hand and operate upon it with another, or to hold a lid up with one hand while he reached inside a box for a toy with the other. This differentiation of hand usage is essential for further development of skilled action and does require the infant to make a distinction between 'holding' and 'operating upon what is held'. Bruner speculated that this same type of distinction might underlie both diffuse and focal attention to objects, and to topic and comment in human language. Thus, for Bruner, the development of skilled action forms one of the bases for further cognitive development.

Bower (1977) has conducted several experimental studies of the development of the object concept. He found that infants of under 4 months did not realise that the *same* object could move from A to B along a regular path. Rather the infants seemed to believe that three objects were involved: (1) The object at A; (2) the object at B; and (3) the object moving from A to B. Between 4 and 5 months infants appeared to understand that the same object could move from A to B. This development of understanding was demonstrated in an experiment by Mundy-Castle and Anglin (1969), quoted by Bower. In this experiment the infant being tested was placed facing a screen which had an oblong opening, or window, on the right side and one on the left. The infant would then see an object appear at the bottom of the left-hand opening and proceed to move upwards until it reached the top of the opening where it was hidden by the screen. The object would then reappear at the top of the right-hand opening and move downwards until it was, once again, hidden by the screen. The researchers found that the youngest infants would either look from window to window, waiting, as it were, for the object to reappear, or they would behave as if they expected the object to go on moving in a straight line and therefore looked upwards to the ceiling when it disappeared on the left, and downwards to the floor when it disappeared on the right. However, between 4 and 5 months the infant began to follow with their eyes the path they (correctly) assumed the object must take while behind the screen in order to appear in the expected position in the other opening.

Bower also found that infants of 5 months did not understand spatial relationships between objects, particularly when two objects shared a common boundary as when, for example, one was put on top of another. If the infant saw one toy put on top of another he seemed to see the result as a third toy and would not attempt to take the first toy off the second. Infants were shown to be equally confused if one toy was put inside another, so that, even when aged 10 to 11 months, if the infant saw a toy put inside cup A, and then A (with the toy) and cup B (without the toy) were moved, so that they changed places while the infant watched, the infant would look in cup B for the toy. In other words even though the infant had developed the realisation that he could search for an object he would look in the *place* where the object disappeared, apparently oblivious to the relationship between container and contained. In another experiment it was found that if a small toy was put in front of, or behind, a larger one the infant was able to think of them as separate and retrieve the smaller toy unless they were touching and therefore sharing a common boundary. Then the infant would no longer attempt to retrieve the smaller toy. This misunderstanding of spatial relations can affect the infant's tool-using ability described by Piaget as appearing in stage 4 (8-12 months). Bower has shown that even at six months an infant would pull a cloth to reach a toy which was on the cloth but out of reach. However if the toy were beside the cloth the infant would, until 10 months of age, pull this cloth as if he would thereby obtain the toy. Bower argued that the problem is that the infant does not understand the spatial relationship of 'on top'. The infant's behaviour, however, could be a late example of the overgeneralised magical thinking found by Piaget to be a characteristic of the previous stage (4-8 months).

Perhaps one of the most significant features of sensori-motor intelligence is that, although there will be individual variation in the rate at which infants will move from stage to stage within the first two years, all non-defective infants will achieve the final stage of functioning. The fact that the final level is attained by all, unlike the functional variability found when older children and adults are tested, led Scarr-Salapatek (1976) to argue that the behaviours characteristic of sensori-motor intelligence evolved before man was split off from the great apes and that, unlike the cognitive behaviour which characterises older children and adults, this particular form of intelligence has many similarities with that of non-human primates. Thus, intellectually, the human infant is more like all other human infants and like non-human primate infants than is the human child or adult like other children or adults, since the intellectual skills that adults and children use appeared later in our evolution and therefore show greater within-species diversification. Scarr-Salapatek also argued that the behaviours characteristic of the first two years are associated with the older areas of the brain, and hence all that is required for their development is that the infant shall be placed in a normal human environment with the normal opportunities for exploration and learning. Only if the infant's environment is very unusual will the developmental stages fail to unfold entirely, although their emergence may be delayed by understimulation. Further, if an infant should be deprived of a normal environment for a time, say through serious illness or extremely disturbed home conditions, his development would be expected to catch up and proceed normally once the abnormality was removed since the long evolutionary history of sensori-motor intelligence implies that its course will not easily be deflected nor its emergence suppressed.

Another significant characteristic of sensori-motor intelligence is that, while no particular form of behaviour is inbuilt, the infant does have an 'inbuilt bias' towards developing certain types of behaviour, for example hand-eye co-ordination. Blind infants have been found to start 'gazing' at their hands at the same time as sighted children (Freedman, 1974) and it must be assumed that the emergence of this behaviour is genetically determined. As Scarr-Salapatek commented 'the opportunity for hand-eye co-ordination to develop has not been left to experiential chance' (1976, p. 179). It therefore appears that the human infant has inherited a 'preadapted responsiveness to certain learning opportunities' (ibid, p. 194). Trevarthen (1977) seems to support this since he argued that early in life the infant exhibits 'programmes of motor action' which are carried out independently of the external world and further that, in a certain sense, intention is innate since the infant actively seeks stimulation, for example by moving in order to see more clearly. These actions are seen, by Trevarthan, as rudimentary intentions.

Despite the overall lack of variability in sensori-motor intelligence several researchers have drawn attention to possible environmental factors which may cause individual differences in cognitive development at this stage and, perhaps, subsequently. Yarrow, Rubenstein and Pedersen (1975), having studied infants aged 5-6 months both at home and in the laboratory, concluded that by the age of 6 months infants were displaying individual characteristics which could be related to discrete variables in their environment. Their major finding was that a relationship could be found between specific aspects of the environment and specific aspects of infant behaviour. A distinction was made between the infant's animate and inanimate environment, the effects of which were found to be relatively independent. It appeared that the emergence of secondary circular reactions (see p. 34) was related to the presence of inanimate objects in the infant's environment which provided feedback. In the animate environment, if the infant had a mother who responded to his coos and early vocalisations, he would increase his output, whereas if she was responsive to his crying then the effect was more general and more likely to increase the infant's motivation to pursue tasks. The development of object permanence seemed to be related to both kinesthetic stimulation and variety in social stimulation. The authors suggested that this was because varied experiences with the mother would enable the infant to realize that the various mothers with whom he interacted were, in fact, one, and hence learn that he was distinct from her whereas kinesthetic stimulation would help him to delimit the boundary of his body and therefore come to give up the symbiotic view of himself and his mother. Exploratory behaviour was found to correlate with the provision and availability of varied and complex objects for the infant's play. The overall conclusion of this study was that the contributions of the animate and the inanimate environments are distinct and are not interchangeable.

Several investigators have drawn attention to the role of social interaction in cognitive development. The Newsons (1976) maintained, against Piaget's view of cognition stemming from infant-environment interaction, that it originated in mother-infant interaction. They argued that the newborn infant is socially sensitive and active, and through reciprocal interaction with his mother he will develop those 'shared understandings which constitute human knowledge' (p. 95). The mother and infant were seen as sharing experiences when they engaged in preverbal communication, particularly when they were both looking at, and concentrating on, the same object. In this situation their mutual and shared understanding was seen, by the Newsons, as the cradle of human cognition.

The mother's role in cognitive development has, to an extent, been explicated as aiding the process of differentiation of self from other, and hence developing an understanding of the subjective self versus the objective other, whether animate or inanimate. Kaye (1977) drew attention to the way in which mother-infant mutual exchanges have many of the characteristics of dialogue, especially its turn-taking quality, and argued that through engaging in this the infant will develop a sense of self which he will then transfer to other two-person situations. Kaye, referring to Spitz's (1964) views, also saw the significance of this early dialogue for the infant as giving him a sense of 'being responded to and having his actions completed in a context' (p. 113). Papousek and Papousek (1977) stressed the mothers role as a 'biological mirror' by means of which the infant learns to associate his own felt movements with what he sees his mother do in imitation of him. So that when he puts out his tongue she will put out hers and the infant will learn in this way both what he is doing, and how he can affect his mother's behaviour. They also found that the infant would only smile if the mother's behaviour was contingent on his, i.e. if she put her tongue out after he had done so; he would not smile if she acted first.

Décarie (1978) showed that the mother is likely to be one of the first 'objects' that the infant realises has permanence, thus paving the way for his understanding of object permanence in general. The reason why the mother is so salient is that she 'activates – simultaneously . . . the different schemes through which the infant apprehends reality' (p. 197), and thus is the most likely aspect of the environment to be differentiated by the infant. Bell (1970) found that, in the group of infants she studied, person permanency usually preceded object permanency. The infants who achieved object permanence first seemed to have a colder relationship with their mothers and were later in developing object permanency than were the infants who developed it after person permanency. Support for the significance of the mother in the development of object permanency was given by a comparative study of infants in a 'model' orphanage and in a municipal orphanage (Paraskevopoulos and Hunt, 1971), in which it was found that the infants in the municipal orphanage were later in developing object permanence. The main difference between the orphanages was judged to be the infant-caregiver ratio, thus suggesting that social interaction was responsible for the development of object permanence.

Communication

In order to interact with others the infant and young child must engage in both verbal and non-verbal communication with them. For this to be successful he must develop the ability to understand what the other person intends to communicate and, in turn, be able to communicate what he intends the other to understand. As Cazden (1977) commented, 'this transfer depends not only on a shared human intentional system but also on shared interpretations of the meaning of alternative realizations of particular intents' (p. 312). As the infant matures he will become partially aware that his viewpoint differs from that of others. However, an awareness of separateness is not sufficient to enable him to communicate with ease. He cannot fully comprehend the way the other thinks, nor can he fully understand what the other is attempting to communicate, since his range of experience will necessarily be both limited and specialised. The infant and child is thus faced with the task of learning how to communicate unambiguously, and how to understand the range of meanings the other is communicating. This learning will usually result in mutual comprehension. Nevertheless learning both how to comprehend the nuances of another's utterance and to transmit one's intentions clearly is a task which will continue throughout life. The difficulty of this undertaking was underlined by Golding (1959) when he said, 'To communicate is our passion and our despair. . . . My darkness reaches out and fumbles at a typewriter with its tongs. Your darkness reaches out with your tongs and grasps a book. There are twenty modes of filter and translation between us' (p. 8).

Communication is both a cognitive and a social act which implies the presence of two or more people who wish to understand and to be understood. It is possible that some of the abberant development, outlined in Chapter 3, may be due either to a failure in communication despite the intention to communicate, or to a low level of attempts at communication between an infant and his significant adults. Similarly some of the adverse effects attributed to maternal absence may be due to the absence of the person with whom the infant is best able to communicate. Certainly both cognitive and social development involve communication between the child and significant others, and therefore communication itself becomes another variable to be taken into account when considering the development of the child's belief in his own competence.

How, then, does this essential capacity to communicate develop in infants from the moment of the first cry to the start of verbal language in the second year? The simple answer is that we do not know. However, there have been some illuminating descriptions of the stages of development based on the observation of infants. Dore (1973, 1974) delimited four stages:

1 *Prelinguistic communication:* Here the infant's intentions give rise to 'orectic attitudes' which communicate his hunger, pain, tiredness etc.
2 *Presyntactic:* Now the child uses words but only one word at a time. The *way* he uses this word has to convey the burden of his meaning.
3 *Syntactic communication:* Words are now combined. In addition he will use intonation and syntax to express his needs.
4 *Speech acts:* These contain both cognitive meaning and expression. Form and manner now come together and the child begins to develop verbal language.

Halliday (1975) was concerned with the way in which the infant used language to express his intentions towards others, that is to make meaningful utterances. He based his theory on the intensive analysis of the language of one child, Nigel, between the ages of 9 and 24 months. At 10½ months Nigel could make sounds, which appeared to have four functions:

1 To express his needs (instrumental)
2 To affect the behaviour of other people (regulatory)
3 To interact or be in contact with others (interpersonal)
4 To show his awareness of himself (personal)

In the next stage the meanings previously expressed by sounds became
embodied in words, usually one word at a time. A single word could be
used for more than one function. For example, pointing out the existence
of an object and expressing a wish to manipulate it. He could also
comment on what he was seeing but did not seek to share his experience,
verbally, with others. Up to 19 months intonation was still important as a
way of conveying meaning. At 18 months dialogue appeared in that
Nigel could ask 'What's that?' and could respond to *wh* questions, to a
command and to a statement. With the emergence of dialogue Nigel had
begun to bring his own system of meaning into line with adult language
and was thus able to begin to learn adult language as such. It appeared that
only when the child had developed the intention to communicate a
meaning of his own would he be sensitised to the adult manner of communicating such a meaning.

There have also been some detailed observational studies of mother-
infant interaction with reference to the development of communication in
the infant. Freedle and Lewis (1977) saw language as developing out of
the interaction of mother and infant in certain specific social situations.
They were particularly interested in the patterns of mother-infant
vocalisations in situations in which the mother would also smile, touch
and look at her infant. This placed language development firmly in a
social framework. In their infant studies they found that male infants with
low socio-economic status and mothers with high socio-economic status
produced more conversational openings. They then correlated the
mother-infant pre-linguistic behaviour with the child's linguistic development at two years using the child's mean length of utterance (MLU) as an
indicator of maturity. Here they found that the infants who closed most
prelinguistic interactions made least progress, and that mothers who
began and ended most conversations had children with higher MLUs at
the age of two. In addition mothers who ended most infant conversations
were the least directive with their two-year-olds. The mothers who were
least responsive, that is those with least openings and closings, asked the
least questions at two years if they had a girl and the most if they had a
boy. These results can be variously interpreted since the data is correlated
and a correlation does not imply a causal connection. It is possible that

maternal responsiveness does affect the rate at which language is acquired, alternatively maternal responsiveness may be a sign of a warm maternal attitude towards her child and this may also affect the child's verbal language.

Bates et al. (1977) in a review of studies of the interdependence of language, cognitive and social development argued that if 'dependence' is defined as the situation in which, 'one system requires input from another in order to derive and build its structure' (p. 258) then, with respect to any two of the above systems, for example, language and cognition, there are six possible positions (see Table 2.1):

1 Language is equivalent to cognition: that is, the one equals the other and they cannot be separated empirically.
2 Cognition depends on language: here the child will be incapable of performing a particular cognitive function prior to the relevant linguistic input.
3 Language depends on cognition: thus symbols would be expected to be used by the child in cognitive tasks and play, before the capacity to use the particular system of verbal symbols known as language could develop.
4 Language and cognition have independent roots and follow independent courses of development even though they may, at times, interact.
5 Language and cognition are, indeed, separate but both derive from a common source.
6 Language and cognition go through similar sequences of development but they do not derive from a common source. Their developmental similarity is because they have had to accept the same constraints and are both examples of forms of 'problem solving in complex systems' (p. 273). They are thus both examples of 'convergent evolution'. That is they have had to respond to similar selection and developmental pressures.

These same six positions can be applied to the interdependence of cognition and social development and language and social development (Table 2.1). As Bates et al. pointed out, many authors, writing of one or other of these relationships, have, implicitly, adopted one of the above positions but have not, explicitly, commented on the possibility of other positions.

Bates et al. are at present investigating position 5 with reference to language, cognition and social development by studying 25 infants

Table 2.1 *Models for the interdependence of language, cognition and social development* (From Bates *et al.*, 1977)

Position	A Language and cognition	B Cognition and social development	C Language and social development
1	L = C	S = C	S = L
2	L ← C	S ← C	S ← L
3	L → C	S → C	S → L
4	L ↓ C ↓	S ↓ C ↓	S ↓ L ↓
5	L ↘ C ↙ O	S ↘ C ↙ O	S ↘ L ↙ O
6	L ↵ C	S ↵ C	S ↵ L

between the ages of 9½ and 12½ months. One interesting finding to have emerged thus far is that the development of notions of basic causality, or means-end behaviour, may affect the development of communication in terms of intentions and symbolic usage more significantly than will the development of more 'static' cognitive schemes, such as that of object permanence. They have also found that the ability to make use of adults as aids in reaching desired goals affects language development positively as does the creative use of tools in problem solving. Since Redshaw and Hughes (1975) had found that gorilla infants, although ahead of human infants on most sensori-motor tasks, neither spontaneously use a stick as a tool nor seek the help of the adult experimenters, and do not acquire language, the authors commented that, 'It may be that the failure to produce language-like systems in higher primates is due to the failure to produce certain kinds of means-end analysis that permit communication to develop' (p. 286).

Two questions of interest in this context are whether a child's development will be affected (1) if he attempts to obtain help, thus showing vestigial means-end behaviour, only to find that the help is not forthcoming, or (2) if his environment is so unstimulating that the creative use of tools is less likely to be a possibility for him than it would be for a child in a normally endowed environment.

The fact that all non-defective children acquire verbal language and do communicate their intentions with, at least, a minimal degree of success suggests that they are behaviours which are difficult to suppress. Like other sensori-motor behaviour a normal human environment will ensure the occurrence of attempts to communicate and the emergence of verbal language. However the extent to which the child further refines these basic skills will depend upon the extent to which his early efforts have been felt by him to be effective and have been encouraged. Communicative competence would seem to require an increasingly sophisticated interaction between the child and adults so that what he intends to say is understood by others and what others intend to say is understood by him. In addition communication about the social and physical world will develop in both form and manner as these environments are increasingly explored and comprehended. If exploration is inhibited then the spur to further development in communication will not occur and the child, having no meaning to express, will not seek the means whereby, if such meaning existed, it could be communicated.

Motivation

A particularly important infant characteristic, which can be seen in the sensori-motor period, is that of motivation to learn. Gilbert (1970) argued that motivation aids natural selection for survival and adaptation.

> Any variant that tended to favour survival (let us say the manipulation of tools for hunting and problem solving) would not be very effective in favouring survival if it depended on pure chance or accidental impulse to be exercised. At least, we would expect that those individuals with not only a little better potential for manual dexterity and neuromuscular co-ordination with foresight but also with an *urge* to manipulate objects for problem-solving would be more adaptive to environmental stresses and challenges than would those who had similar potentials but no interest in exercising them . . . an unmotivated species would sooner or later have succumbed to a well motivated one, just as variants with sex organs but no sex urge would soon die out. We would say that the same applies at every level of behavioural integration . . . (p. 44)

With reference to the human species, the studies of Papoušek and Papoušek (1967, 1969, 1975) do suggest that infants are born with the tendency to find an intrinsic reward in the successful solution of problems. In their series of studies they tested infants of three days, three months and five months. They started with conditioning experiments. In the first of these if the infant turned his head to the left on hearing a signal he was rewarded with some milk. In the second experimental condition two different sounds were given, and the infant had to turn his head to the right or the left, depending on the type of sound, to obtain his milk. He then had to learn to reverse this sequence. Finally head turning was rewarded by the sight of a display of multi-coloured lights. In this last experiment the requirements could be quite complex – for example, the lights would only appear if the infant turned his head twice or three times, or if he did a right and then a left turn. The infant's problem was to discover what sequence of head turns would result in the lights coming on. What they found, in the first experiments, was that once the infants had mastered the task they showed relaxation and smiling. Even when they were no longer hungry the infants would still rotate their heads on hearing the signal and still show signs of satisfaction. The experimenters concluded that 'performance of the correct response plays a larger role in motivating the child than reinforcement with milk' (1975, p. 247). Similarly, in the multi-colour light switching experiment, if the experimenter switched the lights on and off the infants would initially show interest and then become used to the situation and lose interest (i.e. they would habituate). However once they discovered that the appearance of the lights was related to their own head movements they would work intensely and did not show the same loss of interest. The author's commented 'If successful, he repeated his feat so many times and with such joyful effect in his gesture and vocalization that it seemed more like attachment than habituation' (1975, p. 252). Of particular interest were the responses of the infants when the task was too difficult. Young infants would show intense distress and then become motionless and passive almost as if they were about to fall asleep. The authors characterised this state as 'playing possum' or a 'total inner separation from the environment.' The older infants would also show initial distress and would then positively avoid anything connected with the task. These two responses occur in older children and adults, and the second is particularly characteristic of children who reject formal learning since previously they have found learning situations to be unrewarding.

Other studies have demonstrated similar effects, thus Kalnins and Bruner (1973) found that infants would learn a series of sucking responses in order to bring a picture into clearer focus, and Monnier (1976) had infants learning complicated arm and leg movements in order to control a mobile. That affecting the environment was rewarding in itself was confirmed in a further series of studies by Papoušek and Papoušek (1977). The infants were, at this time, also seen to show overt signs of pleasure as they were reaching the solution of a problem even when they were alone. This behaviour was seen as a sign of intrinsic motivation.

It therefore appears that infants are motivated to solve problems for the sheer pleasure of acting on the environment and of reaching a solution. Piaget's view is somewhat similar since he argued that the infant has a 'need to function', by which he meant that once an infant was exhibited a certain action he will seek to repeat it and therefore learns because he acts on the environment, not because the environment acts on him. As Wolff (1963) pointed out Piaget's 'need to function' differs from classical views of motivation, which saw motives as internal forces that could be satisfied in more than one way, since, for Piaget, 'It is the *action* which engenders the *need* for further contact rather than the internal *need* which prompts the action' (p. 178).

Wolff's own view is that while Piaget has shown that, in certain circumstances, the infant will act purely as a result of interaction with the real environment, there are many situations in which a more dynamic theory of motivation, defence and conflict is needed. Yarrow, Rubenstein and Pedersen (1975) gave support to this view by arguing that, while we may agree that all human infants actively seek stimulation, which may well be an evolutionary adaptation, nevertheless some infants show more desire than others to actively affect their environments. This was particularly evident in the extent to which infants showed interest in new objects and persisted in their efforts to explore them. Individual differences in this goal-directed behaviour were apparent at six months and were found to be related to measures of infant mental development.

W.C. Bronson (1971) made an important distinction between 'exploratory' behaviour and 'effectant' behaviour. The former appears when the infant's curiosity is aroused by a novel object, the latter when the infant is motivated by the desire to have an effect on his environment by his own actions. She too believes, like Gilbert (1970) that this effectant motivation is intrinsic and necessary for survival, 'not to be intrinsically motivated to attain effects that are contingent upon one's own actions in a species whose members go out to meet life equipped with little but a neocortex and an opposable thumb would seem to be the height of maladaptiveness' (p. 271). She argued that, initially, the infant becomes aware that certain effects are contingent on his own actions; he is then motivated to have an effect on his environment; and, finally, if his efforts are rewarded he will develop an 'orientation of competence', by which was meant the outlook of a person who had faith in his own ability to act and affect his world and to enjoy using his powers in this way. It is Bronson's view that both the animate and the inanimate environment help the infant to develop the idea of contingency, and of his own effectiveness.

Therefore it appears that the infant is capable of both seeking and avoiding stimulation. He has the innate capacity to be alerted by new stimuli, which in turn motivates him to explore and to act. If he is successful in affecting his environment, exploring and problem solving, the sheer pleasure of so doing will motivate him to continue to respond to new stimuli. However, if the stimuli are lacking, or present but too intense or puzzling, or if the effects obtained are not contingent on his behaviour, he will react with passivity or avoidance. If these frustrating situations are repeated one could hypothesise that the infant's motivation to explore new objects and to act will diminish. He may even actively avoid such situations. Since the infant's mother and other caregiving adults are his main source of stimulation, and since they are responsible for the richness of his inanimate environment, then their sensitivy to his needs and capabilities would seem to be instrumental in producing either an inquiring, acting, infant or one who learns to avoid new stimuli. In the case of both the inquiring and avoiding infant something has been learned: in both cases the infant is showing motivation. The difference is that in the first case the infant's learning will facilitate his further development in that he is positively motivated to explore and act, whereas in this second it inhibits him since his motivation is to avoid distressful situations. Within a few months the possibility, but not the certainty, of future success or failure in learning will have begun to develop through adult-infant interaction.

If Scarr-Salapatek's argument (1976), that sensori-motor intelligence has a long evolutionary history and therefore shows less individual variation than the, phylogenetically more recent, later intelligence, is accepted then the finding of Lewis and McGurk (1972) that infant intelligence scores do not predict later intelligence is not surprising. Nevertheless, if there is indeed a link between motivation and thinking, in that the child's later cognitive development depends on his joy in exploring and acting on the environment, or 'effectance motivation', then a link should be sought between experiences which reinforce effectance motivation and later development rather than correspondence between I.Q. scores when, very possibly, the two forms of intelligence have a different evolutionary history and are different in kind. It does appear (Dunn, 1977b) that maternal acceptance of the child's behaviour, as exemplified by the mother's reinforcing the child's attempts by such phrases as 'good', 'yes', 'that's right' or 'a good try' do seem to be related to later I.Q.

It is therefore possible that a child's cognitive development is affected by the way he has been taught to feel about his own capabilities. This feeling may or may not conserve his initial desire to seek stimulation and act effectively. Once again, it is arguable that it is primarily the inter-personal environment which affects the biological predisposition. The latter is common to all humans whereas the former is responsible for the variation found between one human being and another.

It therefore seems that the human infant, in general, is more like other infants than are adults like to one another. Nevertheless there are indivi-dual differences apparent at birth with respect of activity level and temperament. The infant exhibits characteristic species-specific beha-viour but this takes place in a context in which, usually, the biological parents adopt the social roles of 'mother' and 'father'. The infant is characterised by physiological needs, by adaptability, by a desire to solve problems for their own sake, and by a selective sensitivity to certain aspects of the social and physical environment. Parents are faced with the problem of understanding their infant and responding accordingly. This mutual dependence may have several discrete outcomes: the infant may need X and the parents may (1) interpret his need correctly and give him X; (2) interpret his need correctly and give him Y believing that this is in his, or their, best interests, or (3) they may misinterpret his need. The infant will adapt to his parents' behaviour in so far as his immaturity allows. If what he obtains approximates to what he needs the environment will take on a certain predictability and meaningfulness. If this does not occur the infant will still learn, but what he learns will be that he is help-less, perhaps hopeless. It is in this original hopeful or hopeless orientation towards life that the child's sense of competence will have its roots.

3

The development of
the sense of self

Introduction

In the previous chapters it has been suggested that the infant's behaviour, in particular his 'effectance motivation' which is thought to lead to a 'competence orientation', and his cognitive development are affected by his interactions with his social and physical environment. In the early months the infant's emotions (affect) are developing alongside his thinking (cognition), and he is also acquiring a sense of self. These factors (affect, cognition and self-awareness) are developmentally interdependent although they can be kept conceptually distinct. Piaget and Inhelder (1969) made this clear when they argued that:

> ... when behaviour is studied in its cognitive aspects, we are concerned with its structures; when behaviour is considered in its affective aspects we are concerned with its energetics. While these two aspects cannot be reduced to a single aspect, they are nevertheless inseparable and complementary ... In so far as the self remains undifferentiated, and thus unconscious of itself, all affectivity is centred on the child's own body and action ... from this time on the child begins to react to persons in a more and more specific manner because they behave differently from things and because they behave according to schemes which bear some relation to the schemes of the child's own action. Sooner or later there is established a kind of causality whose source is others, inasmuch as they produce pleasure, comfort, pacification, security, etc. However, it is essential to understand that the totality of these affective events is inseparable from the general structuration of behaviour. (pp. 21-5)

Bruner (1974), in an equally illuminating comment, pointed out that 'the Chinese character for *thinking* combines the character for *head* and the character for *heart*' (p. 14). It is therefore most important to keep in mind the interactive relationship between cognition, affect and self-awareness.

The aspect of development known as 'the sense of self' is a crucial aspect since it determines the infant's 'being in the world' and hence both his thinking and feeling. Individual differences may indeed reflect variations in temperament and ability but, above all, they spring from the individual's response to these variations. This response will determine the person's sense of competence or incompetence and hence his self-esteem. Cassius was partly correct when he said that,

> The fault, dear Brutus, is not in our Stars
> But in ourselves, that we are underlings.

> *(Julius Caesar* I.ii.134)

But it must be remembered that he was drawing attention to a particular instance of a general rule, i.e. that success and failure are not determined by external forces but rather by the individual's reaction to external events. If, then, we are to understand individual differences in response to cognitive tasks it is necessary to consider the development of self-awareness, and the links between this and the development of both cognition and affect since, taken together, they will determine an individual's 'competence orientation' to both cognitive and social activities.

The study of the development of self has been conducted mainly by people whose primary concern is for individuals whose development has not proceeded smoothly. Thus the great psychoanalytic thinkers have indeed developed their theories out of empirical data, but this empirical data has been gathered during clinical interventions, and the point of the theory is to provide a basis for therapy. This clinical/therapeutic orientation leads to some difficulties when applying their findings to the development of the human infant. The major difficulty is inherent in the nature of psychoanalytic therapy. This seems to be successful for two reasons, firstly because of the relationship between the analyst and the patient and, secondly, because the former's descriptive analysis becomes the latter's enlightening explanation. However, both these aspects have an 'as if' quality. The therapeutic relationship is not, in fact, the same as other interpersonal relationships in the patient's life, although the patient will treat the analyst as if he were 'significant others', nor does the patient's view of the world, both present and past, correspond to actuality; rather it is created by the patient as a way of making sense out of his experience of actuality. The patient's position, when he seeks therapy, is somewhat similar to the accursed man in Coleridge's poem:

> Like one, that on a lonesome road
> Doth walk in fear and dread,
> And having once turned round walks on,
> and turns no more his head;
> Because he knows a frightful fiend,
> Doth close behind him tread.

Coleridge: *The Rime of the Ancient Mariner*

In the development of the human infant there is no such 'as if' quality. The infant is faced with an actual interactive situation out of which will develop his realistic or unrealistic assessment of actuality. Nevertheless, through an understanding of maladaptive development it is possible to begin to construct a picture of the course of normal development, just as our understanding of foetal growth has come from the study of the timing of abnormalities. Historically, as we move through the theories of thinkers such as Freud, Klein, Fairbairn, Guntrip and Haan, we are led from a consideration of the more peripheral aspects of the self to deeper and developmentally earlier ones. We find the earlier the writer, chronologically, the later the stage of development considered. This is to be expected since, clinically, the last symptoms to form are likely to be the most obvious and hence were the first to be treated by psychoanalytic methods. However, once the presenting symptoms were cleared up, earlier maladaptions, when they existed, became apparent.

The Freudian background'

Freud's theory of development was based on his clinical experience with neurotic patients and on his own model of the human mind. Early in his career he realised that a neurotic symptom, for example a paralysed arm which has no physical cause, has a *meaning* for the patient and is not just a chance event. As Home argued later, (1966):

In discovering that the symptom has meaning, and basing his treatment on this hypothesis, Freud took the psychoanalytic study out of the world of science and into the world of the humanities, because a meaning is not the product of causes but the creation of a subject. (pp. 43-4)

In attempting to elucidate the meaning of neurotic symptoms Freud's thinking developed and, in some crucial respects, changed over the years. Thus his developmental theory can only be understood if it is seen as part of a much more general theory of mental functioning. Although symptoms were seen to have a meaning it was equally clear that, initially, the patients did not, themselves, know what the meaning was. However, during treatment, it became possible for them to recall certain events in the past which enabled them to see the point of the symptom and this understanding led to the symptom's disappearance. Thus they had in fact 'known' what the matter was but did not know that they knew. From this evidence Freud argued that the mind has a conscious and a pre-conscious system, whose contents are retrievable by memory, and an unconscious system whose contents are hidden but which inexplicably affect the person's everyday behaviour until they become conscious. At the same time Freud wondered why some events and ideas were in the unconscious rather than the conscious or preconscious. His answer was that they had been 'repressed' (not just forgotten for the moment). Four questions then arose: (1) What was repressed? (2) Why was it repressed? (3) What repressed it? and (4) Why did it not stay repressed? In seeking to answer these questions Freud developed, initially, a theory of the human person as being motivated by the desire to get rid of 'energy', since tension was believed to be due to a build up of energy, and tension was uncomfortable for the organism. In addition he saw people as primarily driven by 'instincts' or biological drives, the first and most compelling of which was thought to be 'libido' or sexual energy (that is, the search for pleasure through the general stimulation of the body, not just stimulation of the genital region). Hence an individual's prime motivation was thought to be to seek to discharge libidinal tension. This sexual energy was believed to have both an 'object' (that is what is attractive, e.g. the breast) and an 'aim' (the act, e.g. sucking, through which the energy is discharged). In 1910 he developed the notion of 'ego instincts' which were primarily hunger and thirst. Their aim was self-preservation. He then distinguished between 'libido' (bodily pleasure through stimulation) and 'ego instincts'. Finally he revised his instinct theory once more and put the libidinal instincts together with the life-preserving ego instincts under the name of the 'life instincts' which he opposed to the 'death instinct'. The latter, which represented aggression directed against the self, was seen as aiming to discharge all energy and hence totally remove tension, and thus prior even to libido.

Despite the power of instincts, the person was seen as consisting of more than instincts and Freud came to the conclusion that 'repression' occurred when there was a *conflict* between the instinctive drives and other aspects of psychic functioning. The instinctive drives were seen as having the purpose of seeking satisfaction for the basic needs of the organism (the id system). However the person also had to relate to the outside, real, world (the ego system) and attempt to live up to standards which he had made his own (the superego system). Conflict between the aims of the id and the aims of the other two systems would lead to repression. He was thus able to answer his four questions concerning repression by saying if a wish, belonging to the id system, was incompatible with the other systems it would be 'repressed' into the unconscious, since its incompatibility would cause the person to feel anxiety, and the anxiety could only be assuaged by repressing the idea which was causing the discomfort. However, since the original need had not been met, even though repressed from the conscious system, it would continue to make itself felt and seek for satisfaction in a roundabout way.

In order to explain the meaning of neurotic symptoms Freud also developed the idea of a point in development at which 'libido' was as it were 'held up' or a 'fixation' point. Normally, libido would develop by finding its prime satisfaction firstly in the area of the mouth, then the anus, then the penis and finally the genitals, however it was possible for a person to cling to, for example, the pleasure of oral stimulation even though of an age to find most satisfaction in genital stimulation. Of course if libido is fixed at a certain phase then all subsequent phases will be affected as will the individual's later functioning. To explain this Freud (1916) compared fixation with migration.

> Consider that if a people which is in movement has left strong detachments behind at the stopping-places of its migration, it is likely that the more advanced parties will be inclined to retreat to these stopping places if they have been defeated or have come up against a superior enemy. But they will also be in a greater danger of being defeated the more of their number they have left behind on their migration. (p. 341)

Once Freud had developed the above ideas he was able to argue that a neurosis would occur (1) if an actual impulse in adult life was frustrated; (2) if this actual frustration was similar in kind, and hence reactivated, the repression of an instinctive drive which had taken place earlier; (3) if the frustrated adult sought satisfaction at the point at which his libido had been fixated; and (4) if this attempt to find satisfaction was unsuccessful because of the original repression, and therefore there was a conflict between the attempt to find satisfaction at the fixation point and the system which had originally repressed the instinct in order to stop the earlier anxiety. Thus the adult was held to create a symptom so that he could partly satisfy the current impulse without arousing the original anxiety.

Therefore, out of his search for the meaning of neurotic symptoms, Freud developed a five-fold approach to the description of psychic functioning. Each point of view offers a different type of explanation and they cannot be reduced to a single formula. However they should be seen as complementary. These five explanations are: (1) The dynamic, which sees behaviour in terms of the conflict or interplay of mental forces; (2) the economic, which refers to energy tension and discharge, and is concerned with libido; (3) the topographical point of view, consisting of the conscious, preconscious and unconscious systems; (4) the structural aspect, provided by the id, ego and superego; and (5) the genetic, whereby the roots of current behaviour are to be sought in previous conflicts, repressions and fixations.

Once these basic ideas have been outlined it is possible to approach Freud's developmental theory and the writings of subsequent thinkers since all were influenced, initially, by this theory of mental functioning.

Freudian developmental theory

Freud made two major contributions to developmental theory: the first was his description of 'infant sexuality', which encompassed libidinal development, and the second was his theory of 'object relations', which referred to the infant's relationship with the humans in his world – that is, with people as *he* saw them. This subject is not, therefore, the same as 'interpersonal relations', which implies reciprocity. However, the way an infant perceives his objects is likely to be affected by their actual behaviour.

'Infant sexuality' was a distinct form of sexuality, and referred to the infant's attempts to obtain bodily gratification through the stimulation of sensitive areas or zones. It was not meant to be understood purely in terms of genital satisfaction nor limited to the procreative instinct. It was concerned with obtaining *pleasure* from the use of parts of the body, and should not be equated with the relief obtained through meeting a physiological need. The idea of infant sexuality involved the notion that instinctive gratification led to bodily pleasure over and above the simple satisfaction of a basic need. For example, feeding has a physical (somatic)

function, but sucking is pleasurable in its own right. Similarly while defe-
cation is a biological necessity the process, which stimulates the anus,
may also be pleasurable. The most obvious example, in adult life, is
genital pleasure which is sought frequently by the sexually mature
although procreation is not desired. Freud argued that the infant's sexual
instinct 'libido' had an aim, i.e. to obtain satisfaction by stimulating one
of the sensitive zones (oral, anal, phallic or genital) but it did not, at first,
have an object, so that satisfaction depended on the infant's own body and
hence was 'autoerotic'. However, gradually, external objects were recognised and the instinct, ultimately, had both an aim and an object. The first
phase of libidinal development was called the 'oral' phase and was centred
on the mouth with sucking as the means of obtaining satisfaction. The
infant was believed to make no distinction between his sucking and the
object that was sucked. Once the infant's teeth developed he was thought
to gain pleasure by biting as well as sucking and this second period of the
oral phase might have a devouring aspect as well, implying an understanding of the existence of the object which was bitten, towards which
the infant was believed to feel both affection and hatred. Weaning ended
the dominance of the oral phase, although no phase ends entirely and
reminders of these various stages of libidinal development appear in later
life even when 'fixation' has not occurred.

The next stage was known as the 'anal phase' and was thought to begin
once the child was physiologically capable of bowel control. Here Freud
seemed to bring together two discrete ideas, firstly the pleasure felt in
defecating and secondly the child's pleasure in defecating when he chose
to do so and not when others required it of him. The child's faeces were
also believed to be seen by the child as his possession and his gift. The
stage was divided into two components, one was the 'anal erotic' which
expressed the child's pleasure in retaining his faeces or in passing them,
and an 'anal sadistic' component when he is seen to aggressively expel his
'possession' and hence destroy it. The anal phase was succeeded by the
'phallic phase' during which the child sought pleasure by genital stimulation. This seems to be different in kind from the two previous phases since
children do, indeed, feed and defecate like adults and may well seek the
pleasures attendant on performing a physiologically necessary act.
However, they do not engage in sexual intercourse and the first pleasurable feelings in the genital area are likely to have been aroused during
washing or nappy changing. Therefore they are not directly related to the
zone's physiological function. The child will masturbate at this time and
will, according to Freud, show increased interest in sexual differences and

in sexual matters in general. This interest was thought to lead the young child to the realisation that boys have a penis whereas girls do not. As a result of the material obtained during the analysis of adults, Freud claimed that children explain this difference by believing that girls have been castrated, presumably as a punishment, and hence 'castration anxiety' arises in the boys and 'penis envy' in the girls. In this context it should be remembered that some boys are actually threatened with castration as a punishment for masturbation and, further, knowledge of the practice of circumcision could also cause anxiety in the child. However, Freud's hypothesis was that, generally, children believed that genital pleasure and sexual curiosity might lead to castration. The final phase of libidinal development was called the 'oedipal' phase and was dominated by the 'oedipus complex', which resulted from the pleasures and tensions aroused once the child understood himself to be a member of a *three*-person group, consisting of a male and a female and himself (see p. 114).

'Object relations' theory considered development in terms of the object of the instincts during the various phases which, as we have seen, took their names from the bodily zones primarily associated with gratification. Thus 'infantile sexuality' was concerned with the *aim* of an instinct, 'object relations' with its *object*.

> The object of an instinct is the thing in regard to which the instinct is able to achieve its aims. It is what is most variable about an instinct and is not originally connected with it, but becomes assigned to it only in consequence of being peculiarly fitted to make satisfaction possible. The object is not necessarily extraneous, it may equally well be part of the subjects's own body. (Freud, 1915a)

At birth the infant was not thought to be consistently able to think of himself as separate from the mother. Infant and mother co-existed in a state of mutual unity called by Benedek (1956) 'emotional symbiosis' and by Mahler (1952) 'the symbiotic phase'. Freud (1915) characterised this state as one of 'primary narcissism', since the infant was conscious of pleasure and pain but did not know whether they originated internally or externally. Gradually the infant came to make the distinction between internal and external and in so doing transferred part of his originally undifferentiated feelings on to the dimly conceived external object which met, or frustrated, his needs. For example, the internal feeling of pleasure that the infant had when feeding was transformed into love for the object which fed him, i.e. the breast or the bottle. At this stage the infant was thought to be aware only of the breast (the part-object); he did not yet know that the breast was part of the mother (the whole object). The first stage of object relations was called the 'anaclitic phase' because the pleasure-seeking instincts (e.g. sucking) were satisfied by 'leaning up against' the life-preserving instincts (e.g. feeding). Freud originally believed that the mother's breast was the first love object, and that through loving the breast the infant came to love the whole mother.

> The first object is later completed into the person of the child's mother, who not only nourishes it but also looks after it and thus arouses in it a number of other physical sensations, pleasurable and unpleasurable. By her care of the child's body she becomes its first seducer. In these two relations lies the root of a mother's importance... (Freud, 1940)

The relationship with the feeding mother was believed to be the first true object relationship.

The work of Melanie Klein

Freud's developmental theory was arrived at by working back from the neurotic symptoms of adults. However, since his time, psychoanalysis has been extended to include not only the analysis of adult neurotics but also the analysis of children and psychotics. ('Neurosis' implies that the patient is aware that he is disturbed but is not aware of the cause of the disturbance, whereas 'psychosis' implies that the person's disorder is more apparent to others than to himself.) With this extension of treatment Freudian ideas of the development of the sense of self have been considerably amplified and revised. The psychoanalyst Melanie Klein based her theories on clinical data obtained during the analysis of children (1932). She made two particularly important theoretical contributions. Firstly, she distinguished between 'internal' and 'external' object relations and, secondly, posited the existence of an 'inner world' of phantasy. This was thought to contain its own phantasy objects which shadowed the objects in the outside world. She did, however, retain Freud's theory of instincts. Thus, through analysing the phantasies of her child subjects, she came to believe that each instinctual drive had a mental component which she called the 'unconscious phantasy'. (In this she was reminiscent of Freud who held that when an 'instinct' was repressed it was, in fact, the psychological representation of the somatic source which was located in the unconscious.) Thus if the infant's mother's real breast was actually available and satisfying then the infant would not just be satisfied but would also take in a 'good object', i.e. the idea of a satisfying breast.

Alternatively if the mother's breast was unavailable or unsatisfying the actual experience of frustration would be internalised to become an internal 'bad object'. It appears that Klein, in fact, moved from an instinct theory to one of internalised object relations (Guntrip, 1968). She saw infant ego development as beginning when the single external object of the breast was internally split into the 'good', or satisfying breast, and the 'bad' or unsatisfying and persecutory breast. She called this the 'paranoid-schizoid' position and believed that it was a part of normal, not psychotic, development. 'Splitting' at this stage was believed to be healthy and to form the basis for later discrimination. Certainly, cognitively, the infant appears to split real objects into 'the one at point A', 'the one at point B' and 'the moving object', and to believe, before 5 months, that he can have several mothers present at one and the same time (see p. 78). It therefore seems perfectly possible for him to perform a similar feat with emotional experience.

Klein believed that, in normal circumstances, the ego would identify itself with the 'good object' and the 'paranoid-schizoid' position would give way to the 'depressive' position in which the infant first felt worried about the welfare of the loved object. This, again, was thought of as a normal stage of development; the nomenclature is not meant to imply that it foreshadows adult depression.

Winnicott (1955) called it the 'stage of concern' which is, possibly, a better term. At this stage the infant was able to see the external object as a whole person who could be both satisfying and frustrating, and towards whom the infant could feel both love and hate. Previously love had been directed towards the good object and hatred towards the bad one. The infant, therefore, was held to feel ambivalent since he feared that his hatred of the frustrating aspects of his mother would destroy her, and hence would also destroy the aspects which he loved. He would therefore try to make reparation to her. Parallel with his understanding of his mother as a whole object was the development of a whole, not split, ego. The infant was also thought, at this age, about 8 months, to have a belief in his own omnipotence, i.e. to believe that he could both destroy and resurrect his mother simply because he wished to do so. This does seem to accord with Piaget's stage 3 (4-8 months), which is characterised by magical views of causality.

Ego development

Fairbairn (1952) was influenced by Klein but, on evidence obtained from the analysis of adult patients, he argued that underlying the neuroses analysed by Freud there was usually a deeper, and developmentally earlier, level of disturbance. Through analysing this second level Fairbairn, followed by Guntrip (1968) proposed a theory of development centred on ego development through object relations, and not on the Freudian instinct theory. He believed that the aim of libido was not pleasure but object relations, 'pleasure is the sign-post to the object' (1952, p. 33). For him libido was 'the fundamental life-drive in the human being to become a person' (Guntrip, 1968, p. 119). He argued that the infant was born with an innate attraction towards other human beings. Originally the infant was held to have a unitary ego which would develop normally, i.e. as a unity, if he received 'good enough' mothering but which would 'split', in self defence, if the environment was unsatisfactory. The environment was seen by Fairbairn and Winnicott as capable of being unsatisfactory in four ways (Guntrip, 1968):

1 The infant's need for love is not met and he withdraws (Fairbairn).
2 The infant fears the 'impingement' of the bad object and he withdraws.
3 The infant is neglected or deserted.
4 The infant withdraws in response to his mothers vulnerability (Winnicott, 1945).

In this fourth condition the

> infant becomes afraid to love because he finds that his mother cannot tolerate the natural healthy, vigour of his love needs, so that he comes to feel that he is a ruthless destroyer without intending to be so. The mother is not frustrating, angry or neglectful, but she is not able to stand up to the strain of her thoroughly alive baby and he becomes frightened of this situation and withdraws, and has to spend his energy on inhibiting his needs and all pleasurable tensions and excitements they may arouse, leading eventually to apathy. (Guntrip, 1968, p. 128)

If any, or all, of these conditions were present it seemed that the ego would split. One part, 'the central ego', would attempt to deal with the world through conformity and thus become a 'false self' or 'mask'. A second part, 'the libidinal ego' or 'true self', would remain in an undeveloped state as a perpetual reminder of what might have been, but could not be, because its development was stunted through inadequate nurturance. The third part became the 'anti-libidinal ego' and this represented the person's struggle to exist in the absence of a facilitating environment. The argument was that while the libidinal ego would attempt to find good object relations so that it could develop, the anti-libidinal ego, aware that they were not forthcoming, would attempt to repress the libidinal ego so that the person could try to live without the help of others. Meanwhile the central ego would try to 'get by' through conformity.

Since the one thing an infant cannot give himself is a sense of security, when this security is lacking Fairbairn believed that the libidinal ego would withdraw. The result would be an adult who, although, possibly, appearing to be talented and successful, would lack vitality and be characterised by having feelings of futility as well as by detachment from strong feelings or commitments of any kind. Such a person was observed in analysis as one whose heart did not appear to be in anything.

These people, however, also seemed to fear to find their 'true selves' since their true selves were, necessarily, undeveloped and weak and because their central and anti-libidinal egos had achieved a state of 'living and partly living' which would be destroyed if the hidden, and withdrawn, true self began to emerge.

For Fairbairn the 'good enough mothering' which was required for unitary ego growth had two components: 'a being' element and 'a doing' element. He maintained that 'being' came before 'doing'. (In this he was in agreement with Sartre's (1948) famous dictum 'Existence precedes essence'). Therefore what the young infant needed was to experience a 'basic sense of being' or of 'being in relationship' through a symbiotic relationship with an adult who was available for the infant. Once this was achieved the infant's ego could begin to develop and he could start to interact with the animate and inanimate environment. Through his object relations the infant was thought to develop his peculiarly *human* quality: his sense of self.

> ...the one fundamental thing that matters to human beings is to possess a stable experience of themselves as whole and significant persons. It is ego-growth out of primary psychic unity, and ego-maintenance in internal security, not instinct gratification or control, or even ego-adaptation to outer reality ...that is the ultimate motivating force, and conscious and unconscious aim. (Guntrip, 1968, p. 399)

If these object relations were inadequate at the very earliest stage, the result would be 'schizoid-withdrawal', whereas if the problems arose later, at around eight months, then the adult picture would be one of 'depression' with its attendant anger and guilt. In this second situation the ego seemed to be maintaining itself by having internal 'bad objects' rather than no objects at all. These objects were hated and yet guilt was felt for hating the only internalised human relationships which were available. The central points made by Fairbairn were that the human infant's ego could not develop unless it experienced a feeling of 'being in relationship' with another human being and that libido was directed towards satisfying this innate need for objects.

Haan (1977) also rejected the Freudian instinct theory, which she saw as primarily concerned with control, and concentrated on ego development, with the ego seen as a group of processes whose aim was to enable the person to deal with the world while maintaining a consistent sense of self. Thus,

> conceptualization of processes leads to an organic view of man as using his past, engaged in his enterprises, and anticipating his future ... Altogether ego processes engage the problems of living by *constructing* resolutions to changing situations instead of reproducing learned responses emanating from achieved states (pp. 43-4)

The ego was believed to have ten processes which resulted in three modes of expression (Table 3.1). The modes had distinct properties (Table 3.2) and the person could use any one, depending on the situation, although one would be most characteristic of his behaviour. However, they did not represent final states (thus coping should not be equated with competence or self-actualization) but, rather, they referred to ways of responding to current pressures. The family was seen as the major influence in developing ego processes through the mutual influence of parents and children, with the emphasis on the parents' understanding of the child's stage of ego development. Together with her associates Haan carried out a study of adolescent ego processes and those of their parents. They found no direct correspondence between parental and adolescent processes, but the adolescents' preferred mode of response did show indirect parental influence. In general, boys were shown to have

> more expected, straightforward relations with their parents than do girls. Various aphoristic statements fit the parent-son relationship: coping begets coping, defensiveness begets defensiveness, defensiveness deters coping ... Boys are evidently more reactive to who their parents are, while girls are evidently more responsive to what their parents do. ... Congruent with these observations are the contrasting

Table 3.1   *Taxonomy of ego processes* (From Haan, 1977)

Generic processes	Modes		
	Coping	Defence	Fragmentation
	Cognitive functions		
Discrimination	Objectivity	Isolation	Concretism
Detachment	Intellectuality	Intellectualising	Word salads, neologisms
Means-end symbolisation	Local analysis	Rationalisation	Confabulation
	Reflexive-intraceptive functions		
Delayed response	Tolerance of ambiguity	Doubt	Immobilisation
Sensitivity	Empathy	Projection	Delusional
Time reversion	Regression-ego	Regression	Decompensation
	Attention-focusing functions		
Selective awareness	Concentration	Denial	Distraction, fixation
	Affective-impulse regulations		
Diversion	Sublimation	Displacement	Affective preoccupation
Transformation	Substitution	Reaction formation	Unstable alternation
Restraint	Suppression	Repression	Depersonalis-ation, amnesic

patterns of (a) persistent associations between the girls' affective regulations and their parents' processes, and (b) persistent associations
between the boys' cognitive processes and their parents' processes.
The pivotal problem of family exchange for girls appears, then, to be
their emotional regulation, but for boys it is the effectiveness of their
thinking. (p. 239)

Thus Freud's theory of instincts, although useful for drawing attention to

Table 3.2 *Properties of ego processes* (From Haan, 1977)

Coping processes	Defence processes	Fragmentary processes
1 Appears to involve choice and is therefore flexible, purposive behavior.	Turns away from choice and is therefore rigid and channeled.	Appears repetitive ritualistic, and automated.
2 Is pulled toward the future and takes account of the needs of the present.	Is pushed from the past.	Operates on assumptions which are privatistically based.
3 Oriented to the reality requirements of present situation.	Distorts aspects of present requirements.	Closes system and is non-responsive to present requirements.
4 Involves differentiated process thinking that integrates conscious and pre-conscious elements.	Involves undifferentiated thinking and includes elements that do not seem part of the situation.	Primarily and unadulteratedly determined by affect needs.
5 Operates with the organism's necessity of 'metering' the experiencing of disturbing affects.	Operates with assumption that it is possible to magically remove disturbing feelings.	Floods person with affect.
6 Allows various forms of affective satisfaction in open, ordered and tempered way.	Allows gratification by subterfuge.	Allows unmodulated gratification of some impulses.

infant sexuality, and object relations, has been superseded by theories of ego development which stress the role of the parents and the effects of ego growth on the child's ability to cope with the vicissitudes of life, rather than to defend himself against them, or to enter a state of schizoid withdrawal, which may appear to have short term advantages but will lead to an impoverishment of the person's affective life. The process, therefore, whereby the interpersonal environment affects the infant's 'competence orientation' is that the earliest intimate relationship engenders in the infant various modes of response, or coping strategies, which are examples of adaptation in that they are developed as a means of making sense of the cultural and social environment in which he finds himself.

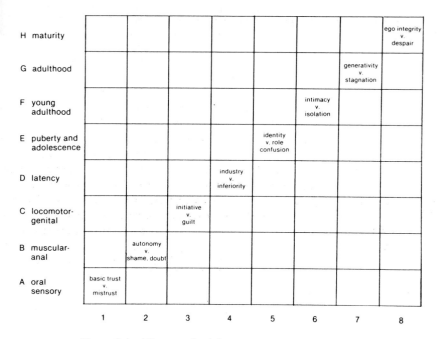

Figure 3.1 *The growth of the ego* (From Erikson, 1950)

Social origins of the self

Two views of the development of the sense of self which are complementary to those discussed above are those of Mead (1934) and Erikson (1950, 1959) in that they stress the role of social interaction in the development of self-awareness.

Erikson believed that as the child interacted with a widening social environment so would his personality develop. He stressed that this development was a function of both the child's level of maturity and the response of others to him. Thus each stage presented the child with a particular developmental challenge which would need to be overcome so that he could proceed to the next level.

> ... in the sequence of his most personal experiences the healthy child given a reasonable amount of guidance, can be trusted to obey inner laws of development, laws which create a succession of potentialities for significant interaction with those who tend him. (1959, p. 52)

Erikson believed that there were eight such 'stages', or 'ways of experience, accessible to introspection; ways of behaving observable by others; and objective inner states determinable by tests and analysis' (1959, p. 56). In each stage the individual was, as it were, presented with a particular choice, and each reached its culmination at a certain period in the life cycle, although, of course, it was not confined entirely to that period (see Fig. 3.1). The eight stages were:

1	Basic trust v. mistrust	5	Identity v. role confusion
2	Autonomy v. shame and doubt	6	Intimacy v. isolation
3	Initiative v. guilt	7	Generativity v. stagnation
4	Industry v. inferiority	8	Ego integrity v. despair

Only the first three stages will be considered here.

It is during the first year that the feeding infant was believed to develop his sense of trust through his interaction with a sensitive mother. In particular it is the mother's predictability which will foster the child's belief in himself and his world.

> The amount of trust derived from earliest infantile experience does not seem to depend on absolute quantities of food or demonstrations of love, but rather on the quality of the maternal relationship. Mothers create a sense of trust in their children by that kind of administration which in its quality combines sensitive care of the baby's individual needs and a firm sense of personal trustworthiness within the trusted framework of their culture's life style. This forms the basis in the child for a sense of identity which will later combine a sense of being 'all right', of being oneself, and of becoming what other people trust one will become. There are, therefore, . . . few frustrations in either this or the following stages which the growing child cannot endure if the frustration leads to the ever renewed experience of greater sameness and stronger continuity of development towards a final integration of the individual life cycle with some meaningful wider belongingness. Parents must not only have certain ways of guiding by prohibition and permission; they must also be able to represent to the child a deep, almost somatic, conviction that there is a meaning to what they are doing. Ultimately, children become neurotic not from frustrations, but from the lack or loss of societal meaning in these frustrations. (1950, p. 241)

During the second and third years autonomy develops. As the child tries out his developing powers he needs the parents' firmness, support and praise otherwise he will come to feel shame and doubt in his own abilities as he is faced by his natural weaknesses. When aged four or five the child is able to walk with ease, to communicate with others and to engage in make-believe play. In one sense he has become powerful, and he needs to use his power but not to the extent that he becomes guilty about the consequences of his activities.

> The danger of this stage is a sense of guilt over the goals contemplated and the acts initiated in one's exuberant enjoyment of new locomotor and mental power: acts of aggressive manipulation and coercion which soon go far beyond the executive capacity of organism and mind and therefore call for an energetic halt to one's contemplated initiative. (1950, p. 247)

In describing the eight stages Erikson took account of the biological basis of behaviour and Freud's psycho-sexual stages, but he placed most emphasis on the significance of the infant's encounters with his social environment and the resulting ego development.

Mead (1934) also stressed the significance of social interaction for the development of self but his concern was somewhat different. He believed that through social interaction the child begins to appreciate that others have a view of him, i.e. he is 'good' or 'bad', 'clever and amusing' etc. and that once he can take the role of these others then the child can look at himself and consider what others would think of him. Once the child has developed the capacity to make itself an object of its own thinking then, Mead believed, the self has begun to develop. Since the self first experiences itself indirectly by using the views of others it is clear that the child's view of himself will be strongly affected by what others say he is. He held that it was through language and play that the child developed its sense of self: that is, through social interaction involving taking the role of one or more others. Later the child will move beyond seeing himself through the eyes of the particular individuals with whom he interacts to seeing himself in terms of how he measures up to the norms of the 'generalized other' or social group to which he belongs. It was also his belief that 'to be self-conscious is essentially to become an object to one's self in virtue of one's social relations to other individuals' (p. 172). Since this self-reflection of others' views involved thinking Mead held that the essence of the self was cognitive rather than affective.

However, if there is a self, which is doing the thinking about others' views of it, presumably, this self, A, must have some attitude towards these others' views and towards itself. Even a young child can say that he is 'good' or 'naughty' with reference to a specific act, but does not seem to hold that he is good or naughty at the time of speaking. Indeed he may be 'good' when he confesses to a prior 'naughty' act. Mead dealt with this by positing a 'me' which was built up out of the attitudes of others and an 'I' which reacted to the 'me'. At times the 'I' will be in agreement with the 'me' and hence is itself expressing the attitudes of others as is the 'me', but at other times it will be opposed to the me – indeed were it not the individual would have become totally merged with society. How the 'I' will respond is thus uncertain. 'The ''I'' then, in this relation of the ''I'' and the ''me'', is something that is, so to speak, responding to a social situation which is within the experience of the individual. It is the answer which the individual makes to the attitude which others take toward him when he assumes an attitude toward them. Now, the attitudes he is taking toward them are present in his own experience, but his response to them will contain a novel element. 'The ''I'' gives the sense of freedom, of initiative' (p. 177). Thus it is the 'I' which can adapt the environment to suit itself rather than merely passively responding.

Clearly Mead is the most socially oriented of all the theorists discussed. His insight into the self-reflective nature of the self is important when considering the development of the sense of self and makes a counter-balance to the theories of Freud and his followers which, while not denying the influence of others, concentrate on conflicts which are internal, and indeed are primarily unconscious.

Early affective development

If an infant is receiving 'good enough' mothering then his emerging ego will have feelings about his animate and inanimate environment and himself. Diminution of affect could suggest withdrawal of the libidinal ego, and hence affective development is an important indicator of the state of the infant's ego development. An 'affect' or feeling is not just a physio-logical event, although physiological changes will be present. It also involves a stimulus and some form of cognitive appraisal of the situation. The feeling itself lasts for a short period of time but may be resuscitated if the stimulus recurs.

Lewis and Brooks (1978) argued that as an infant learns how to act upon his world so he also learns how to value himself and realises that he exists and is distinct from others. They believed that knowledge of 'other' 'self' and 'objects' developed at the same time. The infant was thought to be capable of distinguishing between the 'self as subject' (ego) and the 'self as object' (self-concept). The former involved understanding the self-other distinction, while the latter defined the self in relation to others, and involved both feeling and understanding. Both views of the self were seen as developing out of the infant's intentional interactions with, firstly, the social world and, secondly, the inanimate world. They further claimed that only after knowledge of the self had developed was the infant able to *experience* emotion as distinct from *expressing* it. The argument was that the young infant might feel the frustration resulting from unrelieved tension and scream, but this internal feeling could only be classified as an emotion once he was aware of what he was feeling: a 'cognitive evaluation' was therefore involved. Emotions which need less cognitive evaluation, such as fear and shame, were thought to develop first. The authors held that self-knowledge, emotional experience and cognitive growth are interrelated and have a common developmental pattern, divided into four periods (Table 3.3). The first period is primarily reflexive although the self-other distinction is emerging, perhaps on a conceptual rather than a cognitive basis. The second period sees the genesis of social behaviour, the self-other distinction becomes clearer, there is emotional expression based on previous experience (the infant will cry when he sees a doctor with a hypodermic needle), cognitive development is taking place, as described by Piaget (see p. 33), and the infant learns of his capacity to affect both the social and the inanimate environment. The third period is marked by the emergence of social categories which the infant uses to evaluate both himself and others. Now the infant becomes able to make comparisons between himself and others and to have a wider range of emotional experiences. He can now start to have intentions and to make plans. During the second year of life (the fourth period) representational behaviour was thought to begin, when the infant can use categories such as 'age', 'sex' and 'gender' to define himself in comparison with others. In this context it was argued that transsexualism is the result of a mismatch between 'knowledge' and 'feeling', in that the transsexual, although he knows that he is male, feels female in gender. (Here the authors were in agreement with Stoller, 1968; see p. 100.)

Saarni (1978) had a different view of the relationship between 'expressing' and 'experiencing' an emotion. She saw the thought-feeling distinction as underlying adult neurotic behaviour, and made the important point that, if a distinction is made between 'figurative processes', which copy reality, and 'operative' ones which transform it, then affect is an operative process which transforms reality, thus affecting how we, cognitively, appraise it. Affective development was seen as a process of gradual differentiation which interacted with cognitive development and with the development of communication (see p. 40). Thus, in Saarni's view, the experience of an emotion was intimately linked to its expression. She

Table 3.3 *Development of self-knowledge, emotional experience and cognitive growth* (from Lewis and Brooks, 1978)

Age (in months)	Self-knowledge	Emotional experience	Cognitive growth
0-3	Emergence of self-other distinction	Unconditioned responses to stimulus events (loud noise, hunger, etc.)	Reflexive period and primary circular reactions.
4-8	Consolidation of self-other permanence	Conditioned responses (strangers, incongruity)	Primary and secondary circular reactions
9-12	Emergence of self categories	Specific emotional experiences (fear, happiness, love, attachment)	Object permanence, means-ends, imitation
12-24	Consolidation of basis of self categories (age, gender, emergence of efficacy)	Development of empathy, guilt, embarrassment	Language growth, more complex means-ends, symbolic representations

argued that, during the second half of the first year, the infant became capable of making a social *relationship*, rather than just engaging in social transactions, which he had done prior to this. This relationship enabled the infant to make use of the three basic categories, developed by Mehrabian (1972, p. 369), which appeared once the infant was able to think about social phenomena:

1 Evaluation of persons and objects in terms of positive or negative affect, resulting in approach or avoidance tendencies
2 Judgement of potency or status as related to social control (e.g. dominance, power relations)
3 Discriminative responsiveness as indicative of differential salience of others for oneself

The studies discussed so far indicate that cognition and affect influence each other in that affect is seen as that which motivates and gives meaning to thinking so that, 'all thinking and activity emanate from a background of feeling' (Cicchetti and Sroufe, 1978, p. 311). this view is reminiscent of Brierley's remark, in a private communication to Guntrip:

One thing I feel pretty sure about is that we feel before we think, even in images, that feeling is therefore our means of discrimination as to what happens to us well before we become capable of strictly cognitive discrimination. (Guntrip, 1968, p. 241)

Clinical observations complement experimental findings by showing that similar experiences in infancy can affect both the child's developing sense of self and affective development, thus linking the two; experimental studies, on the other hand, concentrate on the link between affective development and cognitive development. Provence (1978) in reporting her work at the Yale Child Study Center, which has a programme for diagnosis and treatment of the under-fives, showed that developmental problems in the areas of self-awareness and affective development seemed to occur for three reasons: (1) If there was discontinuity in care so that the infant was exposed to many surrogate parents; (2) if the parental care was inadequate because the parents were themselves too disturbed to, emotionally, nurture their infants (in other words, 'good-enough' mothering was lacking); (3) if there was the kind of mismatch between mother and infant described by Stern (1977) (see p. 19) as 'mis-steps in the dance', whereby mother and infant did not achieve initial synchrony in their transactions, thus making their future relationship more difficult. Two of Provence's case studies show most clearly the difference between an infant (Larry) whose sense of self and affective development is proceeding normally so that all his other systems could also develop, and one (Ann) whose early sadness was immobilising her and causing the retardation of all aspects of development.

Ann ...(Ann's) affective development as well as other areas suffered within her two-parent, middle-class family... Ann was deprived early, by her depressed mother, of many gratifying experiences, especially around feeding. The mother's problem in giving to the child, her need to be given to, and her sadistic tendencies resulted in a noxious combination of neglect, screaming at the child, and spanking her when she cried. The child's problem was first apparent at age 4 months... A decrease in vocalization, a lessening of voluntary motor activity, and a slightly diminished interest in toys were the first signs. Shortly after, there was a deceleration in physical growth followed by a slowing in all sectors of development measured by the developmental tests. Language development showed the greatest delay. By age 9 months, she was a small infant who slept long hours at night, had an anxious vigilant

expression when awake, cried at the slightest disappointment or frustration, and was not playful. (p. 305)

Larry: At age 1 month he was described as a large, well-nourished infant
who was visually alert and had the beginnings of a social smile. ... At
age 7 weeks, when first tested, he was visually perceptive and attentive,
and he responded to the adult with much smiling, cooing and
vocalizing... His mother held him comfortably and securely; her
pleasure in him was easy to see, though she had some complaints about
him. At 43 weeks he was a robust, vigorous infant. His record said,
'He is still attractive, vigorous and friendly but there is a change in
Larry... He seems more mature and less of an infant... the
predominant change is in his facial expression which is more intent,
purposeful and self-directed... there is considerable mouthing and
banging of toys ... there is no noticeable hesitancy about approaching
new objects or in giving up the old, though he looks after them and tries
to retrieve them if no substitute is given. This increased interest and
impression of self-directed activity is accompanied by something that
makes one think he has a zest for life. (p. 303)

The implication of the experimental and clinical studies is that if the
infant has received satisfactory care, so that his sense of being is secure,
then, in the absence of any specific defect, all aspects of his development
can be expected to proceed smoothly. Above all he will enter the pre-
school period with a 'zest for life' which should enable him to engage in a
wider range of social contacts and in more complex cognitive tasks,
including learning how to learn, in a spirit of exploration not in one of
withdrawal and fear. By the age of two the child may have begun to
'expect success' or to 'fear failure'. It is this characteristic conscious, and
unconscious, orientation as exemplified by his coping strategies which
will determine his future competence, not any particular experience. This
orientation, however, will have developed out of many experiences some
of which will have been internalised or repressed, and thus form part of
the unconscious which will affect his conscious cognitive appraisal of the
external world and his place in it.

4

The significance of others

Introduction

The first three chapters of this book have been concerned with infancy *per se* and with those aspects of the infant and his environment which are thought to give rise to individual differences in coping strategies and competence orientation. We must now consider the infant's experiences once he begins to realize that he is separate from others and the effect of his earliest social relationships with adults both familiar and unfamiliar.

It is towards the middle of the first year of life that the infant becomes consistently able to distinguish between himself and others and to distinguish familiar figures from strangers. These abilities lead to the emergence of several discrete and developmentally important forms of behaviour: (1) The infant will prefer familiar figures and seek to be near them ('attachment'). (2) The infant will show protest and anxiety if a familiar figure leaves him (separation anxiety). (3) The infant will show fear when he sees an unfamiliar figure (fear of strangers). (4) The infant will, himself, start to move away from the familiar figures and explore his environment (separation/individuation).

Attachment

'Attachment' is seen when the infant, having distinguished the familiar figures in his environment, shows a preference for them by seeking to maintain proximity to them, choosing them as the prime object of attention-seeking behaviours, e.g. smiling, crying, vocalising, and following, and shows distress and protest when separated from them.

The phenomenon of attachment is observable both in man and animals and, while there is no argument over its existence, there have been several theories concerning its origin. The first of these, known as the 'secondary drive theory' or 'cupboard love theory', is based on the prior belief that infants have a single attachment figure and that this figure is the mother. The secondary drive theory therefore argues that the infant attaches to its mother because she feeds it. Feeding is seen as the cause of attachment. Freud (1940) is often believed to have subscribed to this theory, and indeed he did believe that the mother was the first love object because she was the person who satisfied the infant's prime needs for food and stimulation of the erotogenic zones. However as Bowlby (1969) points out, Freud was, in his later writings, moving away from the 'secondary drive' theory and seemed to be suggesting that attachment resulted from an innate drive which would be exhibited despite the quality of the infant's early experiences.

> . . . the phylogenetic foundation has so much the upper hand over personal accidental experience that it makes no difference whether a child has really sucked at the breast or has been brought up on the bottle and never enjoyed the tenderness of a mother's care. In both cases the child's development takes the same path. (Freud, 1940)

Subsequent studies have shown the secondary drive theory to be untenable. Firstly, infants have been found to become attached to people who do not feed them but who play with them and stimulate them (Schaffer and Emerson, 1964a); and, secondly, they will attach to particular people even when they are fed and cared for by many (Stevens, 1971).

An alternative but related view of the origin of attachment behaviour is that given by 'operant-learning theory' (Gewirtz, 1961) which does state that the mother's behaviour is important but, unlike the secondary drive theory, does not see feeding as central, rather the infant is believed to attach to the mother because of her general care-taking activities, including smiling, touching and speaking, not just because she satisfies his instinctual needs. It has been shown (Rheingold, Gewirtz and Ross, 1959; Wahler, 1967) that adult responsiveness will stimulate the infant to exhibit more of the behaviour which has been successful in eliciting the adult's response. It has also been found (Schaffer and Emerson, 1964a) that intensity of interaction is more important than duration, and there can be no doubt hat social interaction is much more significant in the development of attachment behaviour than is feeding *per se*. Nevertheless this theory is incomplete in so far as it stresses the significance of the mother whereas the infant may have more intense interaction with other family members and may choose one of them as his prime attachment figure. However, if feeding is combined with intense interaction then one could argue that the person who provides both will be preferred.

Neither the secondary drive theory nor the operant learning theory explain a peculiar aspect of attachment behaviour that has been found in both animals and man. That is that infants will show strong signs of attachment to a rejecting or hostile but familiar figure (Burlingham and Freud, 1942). Lawick-Goodall (1971) describes such behaviour in non-human primates between the mother-infant pair whom she named 'Passion' and 'Pom'. Passion showed little concern for her infant when she was feeding or learning to walk. She would often leave her behind and usually seemed to put her own interests first. Pom nevertheless continued to seek to be close to her mother, even if this meant that her capacity to explore was grossly reduced. She was observed to hold on to Passion with one hand even when she tried to play with other infant chimpanzees and would continually run along behind her mother, whimpering. It appears therefore that infant attachment is not dependent on adult behaviour in that if an infant can find a friendly familiar figure he will choose him in preference to an unfamiliar one (Schaffer, 1971a), but if the only familiar figure happens to be unfriendly then the infant will still try to attach. Bowlby (1969) argued that infants possess an innate, instinctive, response to seek proximity, initially to any adult, and subsequently to the mother or other familiar figure. Such a response is believed to have survival value in the protection of the immature human infant from predators. Implicit in this ethological theory is the notion of interaction, since the infant must both seek proximity and be able to elicit protection from a significant figure who, in turn, needs to view her infant as attractive and worth protecting. Thus sucking, clinging and following are the infants' means of maintaining proximity. By smiling and crying he shows that he wishes to be close to the mother, and her response to his signals enables the wished-for proximity to be maintained. If the mother does not respond the infant will try even harder to gain her attention since he is possibly seeking to satisfy an instinctive need.

In order to attach the infant must first realise that each familiar person, despite changes in appearance and behaviour, is in fact *one* person and that that person is not him. This, quite complicated, piece of learning has been most extensively studied in reference to one salient figure – the infant's mother. MacFarlane (1975) demonstrated that, as young as 8-10 days, infants could distinguish, by smell, between a breast pad which had been worn by their mother and one which had either not been worn at all or worn by a stranger. In this study the infant was lain on his back and brought to an alert state. An adjustable arm would then lower two breast pads over the infant's head so that his mother's hung on one side of him and either the clean one or the stranger's on the other. The number of times the infant turned his head towards his mother's pad and the amount of time he spent turned towards it in comparison with the other pad was then calculated. In the first experiment 17 out of 20 infants turned their heads more towards the mother's pad than the clean one. In the second experiment at six days of age, 22 out of 32 infants turned more towards their mother's pad than to a stranger's, and at 8-10 days twenty five out of 32 did so. Despite this evidence of ability to distinguish between the mother and a stranger on the basis of smell, at an early age, it appears that in the first few weeks the infant's need for proximity can be met by any adult. This need appears to be similar to the 'need for company' postulated by Suttie (1935), who claimed that the infant's main fear was of being alone and, therefore, any adult is preferred to none. The next signs of infant selectivity are that he may cease crying when he hears a familiar voice, or is picked up by a familiar person and also that he will increasingly direct his smiles to known adults. By about 14 weeks the infant will smile more to a familiar face than to a strange one although previously he had smiled indiscriminately.

Such selectivity will increase as the infant becomes increasingly aware of salient figures. An important question at this stage is whether the infant attaches to *one* person or whether he will attach to several if they are available. Bowlby (1969) argued that infants are biased in favour of *one* figure, so too did Pine (1971) when he spoke of the growth of 'focal anxiety' and 'focal gratification'. Pine's view was that anxiety occurred when the child was separated from the mother once he had realised that she met his needs and that she was not interchangeable with any one else. Similarly 'focal gratificaton' refers, firstly, to the child's finding the mother's presence pleasurable in its own right, so that being near her is an end in itself and, secondly, to the hypothesis that in order for the child to enjoy other activities the mother must be near or at least available, she thus becomes an 'organizer of experience and not merely an element in it' (Spitz, 1959, p. 118). However when Schaffer and Emerson (1964a) studied the attachments of 18-month-old children they found that only half showed prime attachment to the mother with about one third showing prime attachment to the father, whilst others attached to siblings. Similarly, Kotelchuck (1976) devised a series of studies of three hundred infants aged 6-24 months, which included both parents and a stranger, in order to test patterns of parental preference in infants. In these studies the design was for the infant to be, originally, in a playroom together with his parents. Then the father or mother would depart and the stranger would enter. Next, the remaining parent would leave. The experiment continued with one or other of the adults leaving or returning to the room every three minutes. The infant's behaviour was recorded throughout. The results showed that the infants did not distinguish between the parents but did distinguish between the parents and the stranger. For example, departure of a parent would cause protest and diminution of play but no such effect occurred when the stranger departed. In this situation the infant's play increased. Kotelchuck concluded 'children relate in basically the same way to mothers and fathers; early infant social behaviours are directed similarly toward both parents' (p. 336).

It appears, therefore, that infants will not necessarily form their prime attachment to their *mother* but this is not to say that they do not prefer a *single* prime attachment figure. A study by Stevens (1971) would suggest that even when infants are cared for by many people they will attempt to attach to one. He investigated the formation of attachments in infants, aged 4-12 months, who interacted with a number of nurses. In his institution 'during each month of the study every child was fed by an average of 15 nurses, changed by 15, put to bed by 10, got up by 10, and bathed by 7' (p. 138). At the end of six months, 12 out of the 24 children being observed showed 'unequivocal signs of having developed specific attachment' (p. 141), and the majority showed some signs of attachment in terms of preference for a particular nurse or protest at being separated from a favourite nurse. Stevens concluded that attachment is 'more dependent upon the maturation of species-specific response patterns acting mono tropically' (p. 143) than upon the mothers' feeding and caregiving qualities. When the Tizards (1971) studied two-year-old children in an English residential setting, where they were cared for by many adults, they found that these children showed more diffuse attachments than home-reared children. Nevertheless their attachments 'were not indiscriminate: each child had a hierarchy of preferences, as did the home-reared children' (p. 158). It would therefore seem that if several people are regularly part of a child's environment he will show attachment behaviour towards all of these familiar figures, but it is possible that he will single one out as his prime figure. The one who is singled out need not be the mother. Clearly it is in the child's interest to form multiple attachments, since he will then be less distressed if he is separated from one and can use the presence of secondary attachment figures to reduce anxiety when the prime figure is absent. This situation was found by Heinicke and Westheimer (1965) when they noticed that children separated from their mothers showed less distress if even very young siblings were present, despite the fact that these siblings could not perform any of the mother's functions.

During the first six months of life the infant, generally, is fed by his mother, changed and bathed by her, soothed and stimulated by her. He engages in playful interaction with her as well as being frustrated by her when she either fails to respond to his signals or responds inappropriately. Initially, it would seem that the infant does not integrate these discrete mothers into a whole mother who exhibits different types of behaviour at different times. Rather he responds to each as if they were different mothers. Bower's (1977) work on infant cognitive development would seem to support the theory that infants are at first unaware of the single identity of their mother since he has shown that they do not conserve the identity of moving inanimate objects. In one experiment twelve-week-old infants were shown a toy train that was stationary in the centre of the track. The train was then moved to the right of the track, where it would stop, and then moved back to the centre. The infants were found to be perfectly capable of following the object with their eyes as it moved back and forth. However if, after a few journeys, instead of moving to the right it moved to the left the infants would ignore the train where it had stopped previously. Bower's explanation is that

> As far as these babies are concerned, there are two stationary objects, one in front of them and one on the right. They do not associate the object in the centre with the one on the right, or with the movement from one place to the other. When the object in the centre disappeared – or rather moved off to the left – they turned to inspect the stationary object on the right, apparently not realising that there would be nothing there. (1977, p. 110)

Similarly he found that the infants did not seem to realise that a moving object was the same object when it stopped moving. If they had been watching a train moving and it stopped, they would look round for the moving train. In another experiment Bower (1974) was able to show that if the infant was presented with three images of his mother at one and the same time, when aged under five months, the infant would show no surprise and would interact with all three mothers but when he was over five months he would show surprise and protest. It would seem that by then, he had learnt that the same object cannot be in two places at once and that he had only got one mother – despite perceptual and behavioural changes in her.

For the infant believing that different aspects of his mother are different mothers has certain emotional advantages in that he can feel anger and hatred for the frustrating mother and love and preference for the caring mother, so that he can show preferential smiling towards the playful mother and rejection of the one who responds inappropriately. He is thus able to split his world into good and bad aspects and his preference for the good mother is as explicable as his rejection of the bad one. However, at about the age of six months, the infant begins to realise that these separate mothers are in fact one person. Emotionally this is a difficult stage to negotiate, as Klein maintained, since, once he realises that the caring and the frustrating mother are one and the same, he is no longer able to reject the frustrating one as this would result in the loss of the caring one as well. Similarly to love and prefer the caring mother above all other adults requires the infant to accept her frustrating aspects. Thus he becomes ambivalent towards his mother. Yet it is at this moment that he will begin to show a clear preference for her. Why, then, does he still prefer her, and seek proximity to her, once he has some awareness that she will not totally satisfy his needs for protection and nurturance? The answer would seem to be that if the infant's experience, up to this point, has been one of 'good enough' mothering, her positive aspects will have outweighed her negative ones and therefore he will, as it were, take the rough with the smooth. At the same time the infant is becoming aware of the external environment and of his ability to effect it. He is therefore able to start to seek for other sources of satisfaction. Hence exploration will begin at the moment when the mother's position as the sole provider of care is no longer felt to be tenable. At the same time as the infant is developing the ability to integrate discrete aspects of familiar figures, such as his mother, into one person he is also learning to distinguish familiar from unfamiliar figures and to respond accordingly.

The fear of strangers

During the first two years of life infants have been found to react to strangers with wariness and fear, and it has often been argued that the appearance of this apparent 'fear of strangers' is an indication that the child has developed an attachment to his prime caregivers. Undoubtedly aversive reactions to strangers appear more frequently when infants are of an age to show attachment. However 'fear of strangers' is, in fact, made up of several discrete behaviours, not all of which are related to attachment.

In the early months infants were found (Ambrose, 1961; Bronson,

1974) to be wary and to stare at strangers rather than smiling at them as they would towards a familiar person. Some even appeared to freeze when approached by a stranger (Brody and Axelrad, 1971). These responses seemed to precede attempts to avoid the stranger and negative reactions such as crying. However Carpenter (1975) found that infants as young as two weeks would show some signs of turning away if a stranger spoke to them. This was particularly marked if the stranger appeared to be using the infant's mother's voice. In general it does appear that strangers are noticed before they are responded to. During these same early months Schaffer (1971a) argued that the infant can recognise his mother when she appears before him but he cannot recall her image to mind when she is absent. In one of his experiments infants were seated on their mother's knees facing an array of stimuli. The younger infants looked at the stimuli throughout the experiment and did not turn round towards their mothers, but the older infants often turned to their mothers, thus suggesting that they could keep her in mind while concentrating on the other stimuli. It is therefore possible that when a young infant sees a stranger, although he does not recognise her neither does he compare her, mentally, with his absent mother since he is, at that stage, unable to remember his mother well enough to compare the two. Once the infant is able to make this comparison then he responds negatively to the stranger because he has now realised that she is not his mother. Support for this argument is given by Schaffer and Emerson's (1964a) finding that, with younger infants, fear of strangers would only appear when the mother was present. In the mother's presence the infants would look from her to the stranger and reject the stranger. If they were alone with the stranger they would stare in the usual way. Older infants, on the other hand, showed most fear when separated from their mothers, although they would also respond negatively when seated on their mother's knee (Morgan and Ricciuti, 1969).

Once an infant is of an age (6-8 months) to exhibit aversive reactions to strangers both when the mother is present and when she is absent, the question arises as to why he should do this. Schaffer (1966, 1971b) found that the infants were most affected by the stranger's behaviour. They showed much greater fear if she attempted to interact with them than if she remained still and did not speak. He suggested that the infant's distress is because, 'certain forms of stimulation that are generally offered by the mother now emanate from an unfamiliar person' (1971, p. 223).

Bower's (1977) explanation was similar but reversed. He claimed that the infant's fear is because the stranger cannot communicate with the infant in the same way as the mother does, since mother-infant communication has many unique patterns; it is this total breakdown in communication which disturbs the infant. Here Bower is relating fear of strangers with attachment since he holds that an infant attaches to the person who best understands his system of communication (see p. 87). However, it appears that infants do not show fear when approached by a strange child (Brooks and Lewis 1976). Yet the child's communication patterns would also be different from the mother's. Perhaps the size of the adult frightens the infant, or perhaps that adult's communication pattern is disturbing because it is both like and unlike the mother's, whereas the child's is sufficiently different for the infant not to make comparisons. An alternative explanation is that the infant shows fear because he is unable to process cognitively all the new information coming from the stranger (Schaffer, 1966) and thus withdraws as the younger infants were found to do in the Papousek studies when faced with a task which was too complex for their level of cognitive development (see p. 46).

Lewis and Brooks (1978) studied infants in their second year and argued that by this age self-awareness was a significant factor in affecting their reaction to strangers. They compared the way infants behaved when looking at themselves in a mirror, after they had had rouge put on their noses, with their facial expressions when approached by a stranger. Three behaviours, when looking in the mirror, were coded: (1) 'Mark directed', when the child touched his nose, (2) 'body directed' when the body was touched but not the nose, and (3) 'imitative' when the child was 'acting silly, acting coy or making faces in the mirror' (p. 220). Facial expression when the stranger approached was classified as 'positive', 'negative' or 'attentive'. The results suggested (Table 4.1) that a negative response to the stranger was highest when the infants first became aware of themselves, as exhibited by recognition when seeing themselves in the mirror. The youngest infants were the only group to show some positive responses and were also the only group to ignore their rouged noses. As the infants became older they noticed their noses more often and responded to the stranger with attention rather than fear.

Infants, at all ages, have been found to show individual differences concerning the timing of the onset of the fear reaction and the intensity of that reaction. Infants reared in a nursery were found to be less friendly towards a stranger than were home-reared infants (Tizard and Tizard, 1971). However, home-reared children with several siblings showed fear of strangers later than first born children (Schaffer, 1966). Therefore it seems that having a number of social contacts may make the infant less

Table 4.1 *Percentage of subjects exhibiting self-directed behaviours*
and facial expressions (From Lewis and Brooks, 1978)

Self-directed behaviours	Age (in months)			All subjects
	9-12	15-18	21-24	
Mark-directed	0	45	75	37
Body-directed	27	45	38	36
Imitation	9	27	50	27
Facial expressions				
Positive	18	0	0	7
Negative	18	45	13	27
Attention	55	55	88	63

fearful provided that the number is not too large. Brody and Axelrad
(1971) argued that fear of strangers was influenced by the relationship
between mother and infant. Mothers who gave their infants a high degree
of stimulation had infants who were more socially responsive than the
average at six months and who showed less anxiety in the presence of a
stranger. At one year the less anxious infants were more inclined to
inspect the stranger and to show fear of specific people. Bronson (1970,
1971) in the longitudinal Berkeley Growth Study found a clear sex difference when he was investigating both stranger anxiety and shyness during
the first eight and a half years of life. He found that boys who showed fear
earlier than was usual were more likely to be shy throughout the pre-
school and early school period. The girls who showed fear early were, at
that age, more sensitive than the average infant to all forms of irritating
stimulation, but they were no more shy or fearful when they were older
than were girls who had not shown such early sensitivity and fear. In two
cases boys, who had shown strong fearful reactions early in life, were
found to have been hospitalised for schizophrenic episodes in adult life.
Bronson's conclusion was that, for constitutional reasons, males are more
affected by early experiences than are girls. Supporting evidence for this
has been found by Bayley and Schaefer (1964), who looked at intellectual
development, and by Bronson himself (1962) with reference to the
development of attachment and feelings of competence. Commenting on
these findings Kagan (1971, p. 66) pointed out that, in his longitudinal

study, girls were more fearful of strange situations than boys during the first half year of life but more fearful of people thereafter, and therefore the lack of continuity found in the girls behaviour might be because different things caused them to show fear at different ages, whereas this was not the case for boys. Scarr and Salapatek (1970), using the categories of temperament developed by Thomas et al. (1963), found that there was a correlation between fear and temperament in that infants who had a negative mood, low adaptability, low response threshold and low rhythmicity were more likely to show fear.

Fear, however, is by no means the only, or indeed the usual, response to strangers. Schaffer (1966) found that between 30 and 50 per cent of infants, studied at any one time, did not show a fear reaction. Similarly Solomon and Décarie (1976) demonstrated that with infants aged 8-12 months positive responses to strangers were stable over time whereas negative responses were not. This led Décarie (1978) to argue that negative responses to strangers may be no more significant than negative responses to familiar people such as mothers, fathers and siblings. However Scarr and Salapatek (1970) did find stability in fear of strangers in infants aged 6-18 months over a two month period. When fear of strangers does appear it seems to be related to infant characteristics, environmental circumstances and the strangers' behaviour as well as to the existence of attachment figures.

Response to the absence of familiar figures

While infants may protest when a stranger approaches them they will also show negative responses when a familiar figure leaves them. Thus when a familiar person such as the mother departs the infant will protest and his behaviour during her absence will be markedly different from when she is present. In particular exploration will diminish and may be extinguished altogether. Papoušek and Papoušek (1975) found that infants as young as four months could be affected by their mother's behaviour during leave-taking. In their study if the mother behaved normally when leaving, i.e. moved away slowly while looking at and speaking to the infant, then the infant would become quieter during the period of separation (15 secs) but would greet his mother with pleasure when she returned. However, if the lights were flicked off and on, and the mother disappeared, without any preparation, during the moment of darkness and returned (after 15 seconds) when the lights flashed again, then the infant would, at first, show pleasure when she returned, but if the disappearing and reappearing were repeated the infant would start to turn away from his mother and reject her on her return. Papousek and Papousek argued that this was because the mother's behaviour had become 'incomprehensible' to the infant and therefore he rejected her. A response similar to the one they found when infants were pesented with a cognitive task which was too difficult for them (see p. 46). Carpenter (1975) demonstrated a related effect in infants of one to eight weeks. In her experiment she showed the infants their mother's face, a shop model's face and an abstract facial form. None of the faces moved. The infants looked longer at the model's face and the abstract face than they did at their mother's – indeed they looked away from the mother and seemed to reject her. One explanation for this is that an unmoving maternal face is incongruous and therefore the infant withdraws. This, of course, suggests both that infants of under two months can detect incongruity, and that incongruity causes withdrawal.

In the above studies the infant's distress was caused as much by the mother's surprising behaviour as by her departure. More direct investigations of the behaviour of infants when left by their mothers show that many variables are involved. Fleener and Cairns (1970) studied infant protest when left by their mother or a stranger and found that it was not until the infants were twelve months of age that they protested when left by their mothers. In Kotelchuck's (1976) study the infants were fifteen months before they protested when left by either the mother or father. At twelve months, though, they played less during the mother's absence and at fifteen months the same effect occurred when the father was absent. Stayton and Ainsworth (1973) argued that 'insensitively' motherered infants were more likely to protest than were 'sensitively' mothered ones. Infants who were cared for by other adults besides their mother were found (Spelke et al., 1973) to show less separation protest than were infants who were cared for by their mothers alone. However, Dunn (1977a) maintained that distress at parting could be as much a function of the situation as of the strength of attachment between mother and infant, since infants were found to cry more in the laboratory than at home and to cry more if their mothers left them without speaking.

Even though infants will protest in varying degrees when their mothers leave them and although their exploratory activity may diminish, nevertheless the infant, if he is sufficiently secure in his home environment, can tolerate short separations from one of his main caregivers. Longer separations have often been thought to cause permanent damage to the child. These longer separations will occur if the mother or the child has to go into hospital for an extended period, or if the child has to be cared for in a childrens' home or foster home. Certainly in these circumstances the child will show a characteristics pattern of behaviour; initial protest is followed by a deep sadness ending in a form of detachment which may make it appear that the child has 'got over' the separation and has settled down in the new environment (Robertson and Bowlby, 1952). Many dire consequences have been thought to follow from 'maternal deprivation', i.e. long term separation from the mother. However, when a child is separated many things are happening to him. For example, if he goes to hospital he will be separated from parents, siblings and the home environment as well as being ill and in a strange environment. Therefore it is important to sort out which consequences follow from which circumstances. For example, when a child is reunited with his mother he will often show disturbed behaviour, he may virtually ignore her, engage in clinging behaviour or regress to more immature behaviour patterns. Although this may be due to the period of separation it should be remembered that the mother's behaviour may also have changed, especially if she has returned from hospital with a new baby. Hinde (1972; Hinde and Spencer-Booth, 1970) and associates found that, with rhesus monkeys, the infant's behaviour when reunited with the mother was affected by the mother's behaviour. The argument was that separation only harmed the infant if it led to subsequent difficulties in mother-infant interaction due to the mother's disturbed behaviour. One well controlled study (Rutter, 1971), showed that neither psychiatric nor behavioural disorders in children were related to separation from one parent, but there was evidence to link them with separation from both parents when, and only when, the separation was due to some form of family discord, but not when the child was separated because of illness or to go on holiday.

It is difficult to know whether or not early separation has long-term effects simply because of the number of variables involved and the, perhaps continuing, significance of the factors which gave rise to the separation in the first place. However, two short-term effects which have been consistently observed are retardation and distress. Spitz and Wolf (1946) called the condition of infants separated from their mothers for long periods 'anaclitic depression', and saw it as a syndrome consisting of the following categories of symptoms: 'apprehension, sadness, weepiness; lack of contact, rejection of environment, withdrawal; retardation of development, retardation of reaction to stimuli, slowness of movement, dejection, stupor; loss of appetite, refusal to eat, loss of weight; insomnia' (p. 1018). Rutter (1972) argued that the retardation found was due to lack of stimulation, and not the fact of separation, since infants admitted to institutions before an attachment bond had formed have been found to be retarded whereas some institutionalised and separated children were not retarded (Tizard and Rees, 1974). In support of this Spitz and Wolf also found that, once the infants were reunited with their mothers, they showed growth spurts and caught up, almost completely, with the non-separated group.

Two most important questions are: why do infants show severe distress when separated, and how can this distress be reduced? When an infant is separated several dimensions may be involved. (1) He may miss his mother as a person. (2) He may miss the intensity of care which he is used to receiving from her. (3) He may be in a strange situation. (4) He may be separated from all familiar figures. All of these circumstances will contribute to the degree of distress experienced, but the absence of the mother, assuming that she is the prime caretaker, has been thought to be different in kind from the others. Bowlby (1961) argued that the child's reaction is one of grief to the loss of his mother, and is thus akin to mourning. Spitz and Wolf (1946) and many other writers have taken the same view; namely that the distress seen when children are separated is a reaction to the loss of the prime caregiver. Pine (1971) argued that this is because the infant has identified the mother as the person who meets his needs and he fears that in her absence his needs will not be met. Winnicott (1965) expressed a similar view in suggesting that when the infant is totally dependent on his mother, and unaware of her separate existence, if she is absent he will not be concerned except, possibly, by the experience of different handling, but once he has become 'aware of dependence' then he will show anxiety when the figure he depends upon is absent. Mahler (1965b) maintained that until the end of the second year the child is not sufficiently autonomous to live happily, and in particular to take pleasure in play, without the organising presence of the mother, and therefore maternal absence will reduce the infant's capacity to live and play happily. Bowlby (1973) considered two types of hypothesis on this subject. In the first type learning was not thought to be necessary, since here the hypothesis was that, for young animals, being alone is a dangerous situation and therefore to respond to such a situation with distress and protest is a 'basic adaptive response', which developed during the course of evolution to aid survival. The second set of hypotheses postulated some form of learning: either the infant fears the mother's absence because he has learned that his physiological needs will not be attended to when she is not present; or, if the infant associates her presence with comfort and her absence with a lack of comfort, through association he will link her absence with discomfort and hence fear it. Or again, if the infant has found that frightening situations are more frightening when his mother is absent, then he may come to fear her absence itself. Bower (1977) had a different theory. His view was that once the infant has built up a repertoire of non-verbal communication patterns with one person, he will feel totally alone if he is separated from this person since strangers, who have not learnt to respond to his particular form of communication, will, literally, 'not speak his language' and he will be unable to interact with them. Bower pointed out that separation anxiety declines once the child develops verbal language and therefore becomes able to communicate with more people.

It is clear that there are various theories as to why the infant should feel distress when his mother is away. Freud, however, had a slightly different concern. He remarked (1926b) that, although it was obvious that infants felt anxiety when they realised that the object of their love was missing, he did not understand why, in fact, the infant responded with *anxiety* to this. Originally he believed that the infants ego would, in the absence of the mother, be overwhelmed by the feelings which should be directed towards her but which became dammed up, as it were, while she was away. However, he rejected this when he noted that repression was the result of anxiety, not anxiety of repression. Bowlby (1973) suggested that the feeling of anxiety was 'a natural instinct' in many which had value for survival and pointed out that Freud (1926b) may have been toying with a similar idea when he considered that phobias might have a biological role ('the fear of small animals, thunderstorms, etc. might perhaps be accounted for as vestigial traces of the congenital preparedness to meet real danger which is so strongly developed in other animals') and argued that this 'archaic heritage' may still be apparent when man is faced with the loss of the loved object. An alternative hypothesis is that the infant shows anxiety both because his loved object is missing and because *he does not know where she is*. Once the child has developed language and the ability to represent his environment to himself his mother can say 'I am going downstairs' or 'away to X for three days' and, although the child may protest, it would be surprising for him to show anxiety unless he felt some danger might befall her, or him. However, prior to this stage of cognitive development, every time the mother leaves the infant is faced with an insoluble puzzle and his anxiety may reflect the discomfort he experiences when he realises that the situation he is in does not match the situation he would like, but has no idea how to effect a change. He is helpless, and it is the feeling of helplessness which gives rise to the anxiety.

Given that a child will feel distress when separated from his prime care-giver, how can this distress be modified? Both external and internal factors can help the child. Firstly, the presence of any familiar figure, even a young sibling who cannot care for the child, has been found to help (Heinicke and Westheimer, 1965); secondly, the more familiar the environment and the more the child's familiar routine is adhered to the less the anxiety; and, thirdly, the more the child is given consistent, indi-vidual, maternal care by people with whom the child can become familiar the less the distress. The Robertsons in a series of studies and films (1952, 1967, 1968a, 1968b) demonstrated how children who were cared for by Mrs Robertson in her home showed less distress than those cared for in the more impersonal nursery setting. Nevertheless the fostered children did show some distress and it seems impossible totally to remove separa-tion protest and anxiety.

There are, however, considerable individual differences in the way children respond to such situations. Children with no attachment figure obviously will not protest, and children with several familiar figures are better able to cope when separated from one. Children who are securely attached will be better able to tolerate separation than insecurely attached children, possibly because they have more faith in their mothers' eventual return. In general it appears that the degree of distress, and possible harm, suffered by a child depends on the number of adverse factors associated with the separation. A child will show *most* distress if he has a bad rela-tionship with his mother, is put in a strange situation where he receives impersonal care, and if his mother's behaviour on reunion makes the previous bad relationship worse. A child will show least distress if he is securely attached to his mother, if the only aspect of his life that changes is that his mother is absent, and if her sensitivity to him is unimpaired on her return.

5

The development of autonomy

Introduction

By the end of the first year of life the infant's sense of self will have begun to develop through his interaction with significant others, and his cognitive and affective development will have reached the point where, having recognised that he is distinct from others and that they contain both good and bad aspects, he will feel both love and hate towards them. It is at this moment that he will begin to seem to function as an autonomous unit. Although, at this age, the infant will protest when a familiar figure departs or if he is approached by a stranger he himself, when he is ready, will show both a need to move away, both psychologically and physically, and an increasing interest in novel objects. The characteristics of autonomy require that it should be the infant who determines when this moment will be. It should neither be imposed on him from without nor should he be held back when he initiates such moves. Through this process of individuation the infant, while showing responses which are like those of all other children, and like those of some other children, will begin to develop ones which, rooted in his individual identity, are like those of no other child. If during the early phase of dependence the infant has been able to develop the 'confident expectation' (Benedek, 1938) that his needs will be met and that he can affect his environment, then, during the next phase he will be motivated to move away from his primary caregivers, and start to explore the surrounding environment. As Rheingold and Eckerman (1971) pointed out, this separation is of biological and psychological importance:

> It is of consequence for the preservation of both the individual and the species: of the individual, since it confers the advantage of greater familiarity with the environment and thus increases the likelihood of

adaptation to the environment; for the preservation of the species, since it allows the mother to care for the next offspring, and leads eventually to the formation of breeding pairs. (p. 73)

The first sign of curiosity and exploration is the infant's interest in new objects and his attempts to manipulate them. Hutt (1967) showed that novelty in an object will stimulate manipulation with seven-month-old infants, and the infants of ten and twelve months studied by McCall and Garratt (1971) and Ross (1972) showed a consistent preference for complex toys over simple ones; that is, they were more interested in toys which gave them more scope for exploring. Schaffer and Parry (1970), however, found that although infants of six months looked longer at novel objects than at familiar ones, they did not manipulate them more. Once the infant can move he will crawl or walk away from the mother to explore novel objects and novel environments. In their studies of this Rheingold and Eckerman (1969) found that, in the laboratory, infants aged ten months would willingly leave their mothers in order to explore an adjoining room. If there were toys in the new room the infants would move further from their mothers and stay away longer. However, a previous study (Rheingold, 1969) had shown that infants would not explore if they were simply placed in the new environment. They required their mother to be present as a base from which they could move. In at naturalistic study of children aged one to five years out of doors, the children were found to move away from their mothers with the distance increasing as they grew older by, approximately, one third of a metre for each month of age. Mahler (1968) saw this stage as marking the 'psychological birth' of the human infant, and divided it into four sub-stages:

1 A period of 'differentiation', when the child is beginning to move away from his state of symbiotic union with his mother.
2 A 'practising' period, when the child moves away by crawling, but still needs his mother to be available. Walking initiates the child's 'love affair with the world': a time at which, providing his mother has supported his dawning autonomy, the child delights in his own powers and feels them to be limitless.
3 A 'rapprochement crisis', when the child begins to be disillusioned. He becomes aware that he is, indeed, on his own but also realises how weak he is. At this stage he both seeks his mother and pushes her away.
4 The start of 'individuation', when the child is required to give up

his belief in his own, and his parents', omnipotence and begin to function autonomously. (Mahler et al., 1975)

The father and the separation-individuation process

As the infant separates from the primary caregiver, usually the mother, the father may, or may not, assist the child's development. If he has taken little part in the infant's care then it is likely that he will appear as a stranger. However, if the father is physically and psychologically present, he can play a significant part. Once the infant has recognised the mother as a person who both frustrates and gratifies him he will become ambivalent towards her. The father gratifies less and frustrates less and therefore is likely to attract less ambivalence. He is thus viewed more realistically as a person in his own right. He also appears as a significant figure in the external environment which the infant is intent on exploring, having relinquished the wish for one hundred per cent satisfaction from his mother.

In an intact family, in which the father plays a part in infant care, the infant will show preferential responses to him, thus suggesting a degree of attachment. Abelin (1971) reported that the infants he studied smiled at the father by six months and were strongly attached by nine months. During the differentiation period the father may both lead the mother out of her 'primary maternal preoccupation' and introduce the infant to the outside world. His mode of interaction is essentially playful, but in such play the infant will learn skills and extend his social and cognitive capacities. It has been said (Lewis and Weinraub, 1976), that the mother's influence is 'direct' since it is tied to biology in that she feeds and cares for the child, whereas the father's is 'indirect'. This means that the father influences the mother and, through her, the infant and that the infant will hear the father referred to more often by the mother and others than he will hear the mother and others referred to by the father. Brooks and Lewis (1975) found that at fifteen months, while 25 per cent of the infants could label a picture of their father correctly, by saying 'daddy' or some such term, none could label a picture of their mother. By eighteen months all of the infants were able to label the father's picture. Infants were also found to use the name 'daddy' before 'mummy'. The authors suggested that one explanation of this is that the children hear their mother refer to 'daddy' when he is not there, whereas when she uses the word 'mummy', obviously she is present. It seems easier for the child to learn a name under the 'distance' condition. Lewis and Weinraub (1976) also suggested that the concept of 'transitivity' may be important for explaining the infant's tie to the father. By this they meant that if the mother has a relationship with X then the child will also form a relationship with X, regardless of his actual interaction with the person. Thus, despite little father-infant interaction the infant may develop a relationship with him via the mother.

Lamb (1976) observed infant attachment to both mothers and fathers in their own homes. In his study he distinguished between 'attachment behaviours' (wanting to be held or comforted) and 'affiliative behaviours' (the kind of behaviour which could be directed towards any adult who was friendly). He then observed the behaviour of infants aged seven and eight months, whose mothers were their primary caregivers. The experimental situation involved the presence of the mother, the father and the visitor. He found that more behaviours were directed towards the parents than towards the visitor but that the father attracted more of the infant's attention than the mother. In terms of attachment behaviour the infants seemed to choose each parent an equal number of times, but they directed more affiliative behaviour toward their father. It seemed that the parents attracted different types of interaction. In particular the infants engaged in more rough and tumble play with the fathers. The fathers also inhibited their urge to explore less and tended to offer cognitive and physical challenges to them. Biller (1974) suggested that this helped them to develop a sense of mastery over the environment.

Abelin's (1971) conclusion, after his extensive study of the father's role with reference to boys, was that 'during the course of the separation-individuation process, the father becomes aligned with reality, not yet as a source of complaint and frustration, but rather as a buttress for playful and adaptive mastery. This early identification with the positive father figure precedes and prepares the way for the oedipus complex . . . Indeed, rivalry presupposes an empathetic identification with the wishes of the 'other one' (i.e. the rival). It is only when the relationship between the 'one' and the 'other one' has been sufficiently apprehended, that this 'other one' can become 'the one who wants the same one I want' (pp. 249-50).

Resistance to separation

During the separation-individual process the infant will need the support and encouragement of both parents for its successful resolution.

There are cases, however, when the infant, and perhaps others with whom he interacts, appear to wish to prolong the period of dependency beyond the biologically necessary time limit. To understand the difficulties which may arise at the separation-individuation stage it is crucial to take into account the contribution made by both the infant and the primary caregiver (hereafter referred to as the 'mother'). Four possible interactive situations are: (1) For constitutional reasons the infant resists separation; (2) the infant resists separation because he has been spoiled; (3) the infant resists separation because he is insecurely attached; and (4) the mother discourages separation and exploration for her own reasons.

(1) *Constitutional factors which may inhibit separation and exploration*

Mahler (1965a) argued that the first few weeks of life should be called the stage of 'normal autism', during which the infant does not distinguish between inner and outer reality. This is followed by the 'symbiotic phase' in which mother and infant form a symbiotic unit, but when there is also some brief realisation, by the infant, that his needs are met by an outside object (see p. 57). At about six months the separation-individuation process begins which leads, during the infant's second year, to the end of the symbiotic period. She maintained that during the symbiotic phase the infant's ego (by which she meant those mental processes which give rise to an autonomous and realistic sense of self and others) is, necessarily, rudimentary since it has only a dim understanding of 'self' and 'other'. During the separation-individuation process the infant's ego should develop, as long as his mother supports his desire for autonomy and presents him with a consistent and realistic model of the world, so that the infant is not confused about who he is and who others are. But, claimed Mahler, the psychotic infant (i.e. the infant with an extremely distorted sense of reality) is unable to 'use the external maternal ego for structuralisation of his own rapidly-maturing and therefore most vulnerable rudimenary ego' (p. 225) despite the competence of the mother's behaviour. Such a failure is thought to be constitutional, i.e. the result of genetic factors, the intrauterine environment and the birth process. The psychotic infant therefore refuses to admit that he is separate from the mother and yet fears the loss of self inherent in a total belief in fusion.

Mahler based her arguments on evidence obtained during the treatment of psychotic children, but these arguments may well be applicable to non-psychotic children whose ego development has been disturbed in some way. Considerable individual variation in temperament and behaviour has been found at birth (see p. 24) and it is possible that certain behaviours are more facilitative of ego development than others. For example, an infant's constitutional ability to withstand internal stress and filter out excessive external stimuli, together with an ability to wait for the gratification of his needs, will make it much easier for him to build up a coherent picture of himself in his environment, and hence wish to initiate independent exploration. An infant swept about by internal tensions and over-intense, external stimuli, however, is likely to have difficulty in coming to terms with reality.

(2) *The infant resists separation because he has been spoiled*

As Bowlby (1973) pointed out the spoiling hypothesis has had 'wide popularity', but 'no evidence of substance has ever been presented to support the theory that anxious attachment is a result of an excess of parental affection' (p. 277). However Freud (1905) certainly believed that the more the child is given the more he will want, with the result that he will fail to mature normally. Spitz (1965) has an interesting explanation for the kind of empirical observations which may have given rise to Freud's support of the idea of spoiling. Spitz notes that Soto (1937) had observed that 'three-month colic' 'did not occur in infant raised in institutions whereas it was common in infants raised at home.' ('Three-month colic' is a condition in which infants, aged three weeks to three months, will cry for a regular period each day whilst showing signs of pain. A feed will only quieten them for a brief period. At approximately three months the condition seems to clear up spontaneously.) Soto believed that the reason for the difference between the institutionalised had the home-reared infants was that the infants were not 'spoiled' in the institution, i.e. given extra feeds, picked up etc. Spitz, on the basis of his observations, claimed that two factors had to be present before three-month colic developed. One was a physical condition 'congenital hypertonicity' (i.e. tight muscles, especially in the stomach), the other was an over-solicitous mother who tended to respond to any sign of discomfort in her infant by feeding him, thus setting up a vicious circle of stomach cramp, leading to screaming, leading to feeding, leading to more stomach cramp. At three months, Spitz argued, the mother is less likely to feed the infant at every opportunity and the infant has also developed other means of discharging tension besides screaming. Here again we can see how both a constitutional factor (hypertonicity) and an external factor (over-solicitous mothering) interact to produce a particular form of infant behaviour.

Bowlby (1973) also drew attention to the fact that excessive parental affection may also mask hostility towards the child or a disturbance in parental attachment, in that the parents may themselves desire to cling to the child. Since a child will respond as readily to covert behaviour as he will to overt it is not surprising that, in these circumstances, a child may seem unable to separate.

(3) *The infant resists separation because he is insecurely attached*

It is essential, for separation and exploration to begin, that the infant shall have realised that his mother will care for him and meet a major proportion of his needs. If he has not experienced sensitive caregiving he will not realise that he is able to affect his environment, and therefore will not be motivated to explore further; in the same way if his mother's negative qualities seem to outweigh her positive ones the infant will expect the environment to be equally negative. The infant's original attachment, even to an uncaring mother, may well be 'dependent upon the maturation of species-specific response patterns' (Stevens, 1971, p. 143). However, once the infant has reached the point of initiating the separation-individuation process the way in which he will approach it will, necessarily, be influenced by the way in which his former needs have been met. If they have not been adequately dealt with he will continue to seek satisfaction and may, therefore, appear to be more strongly attached than an infant who has passed through the stage of primary attachment and begun to explore the widening environment. There is, however, a considerable difference between the clinging infant who has no 'confident expectation' in his mother's availability and hence dare not leave her for fear that he will lose the little that he has, and the securely attached child who, while still preferring his mother, is able to cope with his ambivalence towards her and is therefore free to seek new experiences. It is as if the first infant feels that should he leave his mother she may disappear for ever and he will be abandoned, whereas the second believes that, imperfect as she is, she does care enough for him to be there on his return.

A study by Salter-Ainsworth, Bell and Stayton (1971) neatly demonstrated the interrelationship of attachment, exploration and maternal care. Here the researchers, as part of their extended study of mother-infant interaction, most of which had taken place in the infants' homes, devised an experiment to assess individual differences in, firstly, the extent to which infants required their mother to be present as a secure base before they would explore; secondly, strength of reaction to strangers; and, thirdly, their response to brief separation from the mother.

The nature of the balance between attachment and exploration and the factors which would tip it were of major interest. In their experiment there were several distinct episodes. Firstly, the mother and her one-year-old infant were put together in a strange room containing toys. The extent to which the infant would explore the room and the toys, with his mother present, was noted. Secondly, a stranger would enter the room, speak to the mother and then approach and attempt to play with the infant. Thirdly, the mother would leave the room, thus leaving the infant in the somewhat stressful situation of being alone with the stranger. Fourthly, the mother would return and the stranger would slip out. The mother would then, fifthly, encourage the infant to play with the toys. Once he was playing she would say 'good-bye' and leave so that he was completely alone in the room. Sixthly, the stranger would enter the room and attempt to play with the infant and, finally, the mother would return.

The results showed that the infants displayed a considerable range of 'attachment behaviours', as assessed by their behaviour when the mother returned as well as their response to the absence of the mother and/or the presence of the stranger. The infants' behaviour was found to relate to various forms of maternal care. In particular the degree to which the infant sought or avoided proximity to and/or attempted to maintain or break off contact with the mother in the experimental situation was found to correlate with four measures of maternal behaviour, on which the mothers were rated on the basis of their behaviour during the home visits which had occurred regularly throughout the preceding year. The first measure was one of 'sensitivity-insensitivity' which quantified the extent to which the mother was able to interpret her infant's wishes correctly as compared with the mother whose treatment of her infant reflected her own moods, wishes and needs, and did not take account of his. Secondly, the degree to which the mother accepted or rejected her infant was assessed. The third scale noted whether the mother interfered in the infant's activities and tried to impose her will, or respected his autonomy and therefore tried not to interfere in, or interrupt, his activities. The fourth reflected the degree to which the mother made herself accessible to her infant or tended to ignore him because her own activities monopolised her time. It was found that about one third of the sample represented normal harmonious mother-infant relationships in which the mother was sensitive, accepting, non-interfering and accessible and the infant, in turn, explored freely whilst using the mother as a base. When these infants were stressed they showed heightened attachment behaviour and thus, for them, stress tipped the balance from exploration to attachment. Whilst harmonious mother-infant relationships presented a fairly homogeneous picture, discordant relationships showed more diversity both in maternal handling and in infant response. One group of mothers were characteristically inconsistent on all measures. Their infants would, not surprisingly, sometimes use their mothers as a base for exploring and sometimes not. They would, however, explore when stressed, which the researchers interpreted as defensive behaviour, and they showed less attachment behaviour upon reunion with their mothers. Rejected infants avoided their mothers when stressed and showed little or no desire for attachment. It seemed that the infant had learnt to defend himself at home by avoiding his rejecting mother, through engaging in independent play, and therefore used the same system of defence when under stress outside the home. Those infants who had accepting but interfering mothers appeared to be the most insecure of all, both at home and in the experimental situation, showing distress at separation and ambivalence when the mother returned. If the mother was accepting but ignored her infant's needs then the infant appeared passive and easily distressed. Since these accepted but ignored infants characteristically received little feedback from their mothers they were inhibited when exploring and could not cope with stress: when the mother returned they seemed both to want to attach to her and to reject contact with her.

The authors concluded that all the infants showed attachment, or defensively denied it, but that their form of attachment was affected by their mothers' treatment of them. Given the small size of the sample (23 infants) these results are striking for the diversity of behaviours recorded, but the findings are in general agreement with the hypothesis that exploratory behaviour, which is so important for cognitive and social development, is affected by the form of attachment which has developed through the interaction of the infant and his main caregiver. Of particular interest is the apparently defensive measures taken by the infants with insensitive and rejecting mothers, which could be interpreted as an adequate means of coping with the situation (but see p. 106). The behaviour of these infants has some of the qualities of the defence mentioned by Hudson (1966) of 'taking refuge from people in things'. He believed that this form of defence would result in a person who displayed the characteristic of a 'converger' of whom he said: 'Two of his characteristics seem to me to stand out from the evidence. The first is his concentration upon the impersonal aspects of his culture, both in school and out. The second, the caution with which he expresses his feelings' (p. 84).

Although it is unwise to extrapolate from studies of children of one age group to those of another, Bowlby's (1973) analysis of the dynamics of

Table 5.1 *Relationship of maternal behaviour and infant response to stress and separation* (Adapted from Salter-Ainsworth, Bell and Stayton, 1971)

Maternal behaviour	Sensitive	Inconsistently sensitive	Insensitive	Insensitive	Insensitive
	Accepting	Sometimes inaccessible	Rejecting	Accepting	Accepting
	Non-interfering	Sometimes interfering		Interfering	Non-interfering
	Accessible			Accessible	Ignoring
Infant response	Exploration	Sometimes used mother as base	Minimal distress when separated	The most insecure	Passive and easily distressed
	Distress at separation	Sometimes independent exploration	Independent exploration		Some desire to attach on reunion
	Heightened attachment on return	Explores under stress (suggestion of defence)	Avoided proximity on reunion		
		Less attachment behaviour on reunion	Used play as a substitute for maternal care		

school refusal is at least worth considering with reference to the lack of exploratory behaviour in insecurely attached infants. His argument was that the child who appears to be afraid of going to school is, in fact, afraid of leaving home and is, therefore, showing similar symptoms to those of agoraphobics. On the basis of his clinical experience with children who refused to go to school Bowlby maintained that they can be

> understood as the products of one or more of four main patterns of family interaction:
> *Pattern A* Mother, or more rarely, father, is a sufferer from chronic anxiety regarding attachment figures and retains the child at home to be a companion.
> *Pattern B* The child fears that something dreadful may happen to mother, or possibly father, while he is at school and so remains at home to prevent it happening.
> *Pattern C* The child fears that something dreadful may happen to himself if he is away from home and so remains at home to prevent that happening.
> *Pattern D* Mother, or more rarely, father fears that something dreadful will happen to the child while he is at school and so keeps him at home. (pp. 303-4)

These patterns can be applied to the infant: Pattern A reflects the situation in which the mother attaches to her child; Pattern B could occur if the infant feels hostility towards its mother (as exemplified by ambivalent behaviour towards her similar to that seen in the Salter-Ainsworth, Bell and Stayton study) and therefore fears that his hostility may destroy her. In support of this Klein (1932) found evidence of hostility leading to anxious attachment during her clinical work with young children. Pattern D is less applicable to infants, except in a diffuse way, since it is unlikely that infants would be able to conceive of a particular external danger. Rather all strange situations may cause heightened anxiety and hence reduce exploration while increasing attachment. Pattern D could be a realistic response for parents of young children (e.g. exploring a main road could be fatal) but if the parents' anxiety when the child explores is inappropriate in a particular context then it would be justifiable to see the child's anxious attachment as a result of the parental anxiety.

(4) *The mother discourages separation and exploration for her own reasons*

As has been suggested above (patterns A and D) the infant's refusal to separate may be a function of the mother's behaviour rather than his own. A mother may well view her infant's early strivings towards autonomy with ambivalence. Thus a mother who was competent and felt fulfilled during the height of the symbiotic phase may inhibit separation and individuation in an attempt to prolong this rewarding period. She may well do much more than is necessary for her infant. If the infant complies, and if the relationship is otherwise healthy he may appear to be 'overdependent' (Stendler, 1954) in terms of doing things for himself but will not, otherwise, show signs of anxious attachment. A much more serious situation is when the mother reverses roles and attaches to her child possibly because she was insecurely attached to her own mother. Bowlby (1973) describes such a situation thus:

> the parent concerned is found to be intensely anxious about the availability of her own attachment figures and unconsciously to be inverting the normal parent-child relationship by requiring the child to be the parent figure and adopting the role of child herself. Thus the child is expected to care for the parent and the parent seeks to be cared for and comforted by the child. As a rule the inversion is camouflaged. Mother claims that the person who is in special need of care and protection, and who is receiving it, is the child . . . In effect what is happening is very different and much sadder. Unknown to herself mother (or father) is seeking belated satisfaction of her desire for the loving care she either never had as a child or perhaps lost, and, simultaneously, is preventing the child from taking part in play or school activities with his peers. So far from being 'over-indulged' such children are chronically frustrated and, because allegedly given everything, are not even free to expostulate. (pp. 305-6)

Stoller (1968), writing of his clinical work with patients suffering from sexual and gender disturbances, drew attention to an extreme form of maternal attachment and its effects. In considering certain cases of male disturbance he argued that it is necessary to distinguish between 'transsexuals', and 'transvestites': the latter are sure that they are sexually male and have no wish to change their gender. What they enjoy is being dressed in female clothes whilst knowing that they are, in fact, male. A transsexual however, whilst accepting that, physically, he belongs to the male sex feels that he ought to be female. In other words he is not satisfied with his gender identity, feeling that he is really a female trapped in a male body. Stoller argued that one cause of a boy's wishing to be a girl is that the mother has prolonged the symbiotic phase and has, intentionally, albeit unconsciously, feminised him. He described the case of a transsexual boy whose relationship with his mother exemplified an extreme form of prolonged symbiosis.

> He had sat or lain enfolded in her body for much of the first year of his life and later, as he became mobile, he was permitted to share her body with her as though it was his own . . . From birth to two whether awake or asleep, he was always with her . . . He was never separated from the sight of her for more than a few minutes. (p. 111)

In considering this case Stoller's line of reasoning was similar to Bowlby's, since he argued that this mother feminised her son because of deficiencies in her own family, whereby she was inconsistently treated by a father who preferred her brothers and received minimal attention from her emotionally empty mother. This left her with hostile feelings towards males and the wish to use her son as a substitute for the mother she felt she had never had. In general if a male infant has been unable to separate himself from his mother then a belief that he shares her gender seems understandable.

Over-intense interaction between a father and child can also lead to a pathological outcome. Sprince (1972) reported a case of pseudo-dementia in a thirteen-year-old boy. Here there had been extended physical contact between father and son in the early years largely due to the mother being ill and unable to care for the child. Sprince suggested that this prolonged physical contact led to a form of identification between the father and son in which the son found himself unable to conceive of his being separate from the father.

Non-autonomous functioning

A serious consequence of failure of the separation-individuation stage is that the infant may fail to learn to interpret his own interior states correctly since the mother has tended to act for him and to live through him. Bruch (1974) stressed the role of the family in creating children who are obese or anorexic. On the basis of forty years' experience with individuals who have eating disorders, she argued that her patients

> experience themselves as not being in control of their behaviour, needs, and impulses, as not owning their own bodies, as not having a centre of gravity within themselves. Instead they feel under the influence and direction of external forces. They act as if their body and behaviour were the product of other people's influences and actions. From detailed

reconstructions of their developmental histories it could be recognized
that they had certain distorting experiences in common, namely,
absence or paucity of appropriate and confirming responses to signals
indicating their needs and other forms of self-expression. (p. 55)

In order to account for this disturbance in self-perception she posited a
two-factor theory which, like Spitz's (see p. 94) stressed the crucial role of
interaction between mother and infant behaviours.

From birth on, *two* basic forms of behaviour must be differentiated,
namely behaviour *initiated* in the infant, and behaviour in *response* to
stimuli from the outside . . . the mother's behaviour in relation to the
child is either *responsive or stimulating.* The interaction between the
environment and the infant can be rated as *appropriate* or *inappropriate*, depending on whether it serves his survival and development or
disregards or distorts it . . . This theoretical frame goes beyond, or
avoids, the traditional dichotomy of somatic and psychological aspects
of development. An infant handicapped by genetic factors, or suffering
from paranatal injuries or confusing earliest experiences, is apt to give
clues to his needs that are weak, indistinct, or contradictory. It would
be a difficult task for any mother to satisfy them appropriately, and will
be completely confusing to a mother who herself is emotionally disturbed, preoccupied with her own problems, and impervious to
expressions of a child's needs. (p. 55)

She found that in the families of her patients the parents imposed their
meanings and constructions of situations onto the child by 'direct
mislabelling of a child's feeling state, such as that he *must* be hungry (or
cold or tired), regardless of the child's own experience' (p. 62), with the
result that the child 'comes to mistrust the legitimacy of his own feelings
and experiences' (p. 62). If a child complies with this maternal imposition
of her concept of his needs then, obviously, he will become over-dependent since he will fail to develop a secure sense of himself as an active,
effective individual. Such children were found to become obese, or schizophrenic, or both. The families of anorexics often seemed to have been
happy and functioning well before the onset of the child's illness. However, further study revealed a pattern in which, often in a subtle way, the
child's autonomy was consistently blocked. Bruch interpreted these
children's subsequent anorexia as 'a desperate struggle for a self-respect-
ing identity' (p. 250), despite the fact that they seemed beset with a 'para-
lysing sense of ineffectiveness . . . They experience themselves as acting

only *in response* to demands coming from other people in situations, and not as doing things because *they want to*'. One girl, during treatment, reported with delight her realisation that she wore wellingtons to keep her feet dry and not because her mother would frown if she didn't. It is interesting to note in this context the view of Yarrow (see p. 32) that disturbances at one stage of development will often show up at a similar psychological stage, not in the next chronological period. Typically anorexia occurs in adolescence, that is at the time of puberty when the child is required, once again, to separate from the parents and take up autonomous functioning as a sexually mature person capable of leaving home and choosing a career. Such autonomous choice is impossible for the child who has existed in a state of unthinking compliance to parental domination.

Children who are overtly rejected by their parents have been found by several investigators to be characterised by emotional withdrawal and underachievement and, in some cases, to be neurotic (Wolberg, 1944; Siegelman, 1966; Slater, 1962; Jacobs et al., 1972). Since neurosis implies the inappropriate use of defence mechanisms to avoid anxiety aroused by the reactivation of earlier psychic conflicts it is now necessary to consider the role of defence in development.

It is said that 'there's no harm in wishing', but unfulfilled wishes can lead to considerable amounts of pain and guilt, particularly if the very wish is felt by the individual to be unacceptable. Many infant impulses are initially pleasurable but become unacceptable to the ego once the moral standards of adults have been internalised. The ego can thus protect itself by trying to avoid the arousal of dangerous impulses by means of the 'inhibitory defences', or it may attempt to distort the aroused impulses by 'repressive' defences (Madison, 1961). Freud (1915b) called the two 'inhibitory defences', of emotional and behavioural inhibition, 'repression' but made it clear that he felt they differed from the true repressive defences in which the impulse existed but was distorted. Emotional and behavioural inhibition can be achieved if a person avoids situations which might arouse the dangerous impulses, and this is the basis of many phobias. However, both true repression and the avoidance of danger by inhibition are unsuccessful defences since the wish remains unsatisfied and energy will be used in dealing with it. A successful defence is one in which the impulse itself is changed and therefore, as it were, defused. The successful defence most often referred to by Freud was that of sublimation by means of which the impulse is changed into an activity which has cultural approval, for example artistic work. He believed that this defence would not be used until the beginning of the latency period. Both normal and neurotic people use unsuccessful defences. The observable difference between the two is the extent to which such defences are employed and the relative strength of their debilitating effects.

Freud's interest in defence was primarily with reference to the libidinal impulses, which are repressed during childhood but which can be reactivated in adult life. Nevertheless, as Glidewell (1961) pointed out,

> It happens that many human desires, and most of the obstacles to their fulfillment, originate in social arrangements. Girls are not born to want a particular type of husband. Children do not, by nature, dislike their parents. Men never inherit the hope of being merchants, or machinists or teachers. People acquire such wishes and intentions as a consequence of living with others. Similarly it is other people, their interests, preferences, and relations to us, which often prevent our doing as we would like. (p. 5)

Although Freud (1929) expressed a similar sounding argument its meaning may be very different. However, it is true that children are often frustrated in their wishes for material goods or certain types of experience, for example watching a particular television programme. They may react to these frustrations defensively rather than by overtly protesting or recognising and accepting the frustration. Therefore defences may protect the ego both from the pain of unacceptable impulses and the pain of frustrated everyday desires. Everyday frustration may, of course, reactivate in the child, as well as the adult, previously repressed impulses or affects.

Sooner or later all children will be faced with situations which cause psychological 'pain' and Anna Freud (1937) made an important distinction when she said that it was the task of education, not analysis, to enable the child to tolerate such pain:

> When the ego has taken its defensive measures against an affect for the purpose of avoiding 'pain', something more besides analysis is required to annul them, if the result is to be permanent. The child must learn to tolerate larger and larger quantities of 'pain' without immediately having recourse to his defence mechanisms. It must, however, be admitted that theoretically it is the business of education rather than of analysis to teach him this lesson. (p. 69)

The defence mechanisms isolated by Freud were: regression, repression, reaction formation, isolation, undoing, projection, introjection (identification), turning against the self, reversal, and sublimation. These were seen by Anna Freud (1937) as defences against the 'eruption of undesired wishes'. She delimited three further defences against 'objective' pain: denial in fantasy, denial in act and restriction of the ego (or inhibition).

'Repression' simply means that the unacceptable wish is not allowed to become conscious. Although it is listed as a defence, it is more diffuse than the other defences and is often used in conjunction with another. In its most particular sense it means amnesic forgetting. In 'regression' pain is avoided by returning to a more infantile mode of impulse gratification. The behaviour exhibited will lessen the pain for a time, thus sleep can be a defence against depression. 'Reaction-formation' turns hate to apparent love: a child who feels hostility towards a sibling may display excessive tenderness and believe that this is the emotion he really feels. Likewise a mother may deny hostility towards her child by over-solicitude. 'Isolation' attempts to deal with the prohibited impulses by removing them from their context. The defensive person will engage in actions which appear harmless except for their obsessional quality. 'Projection' and 'introjection' lead the person respectively to attribute to others feelings he finds unacceptable in himself or, for example, to behave aggressively when he believes that others are about to attack him. Alternatively he may identify with the aggressor. 'Turning against the self' has the effect of turning aggressive impulses which cannot be allowed to be directed towards others on the self, giving rise to obscure symptoms or suicide. In 'reversal' the person phantasises that the situation is the reverse of what it actually is: the child maintains he is loved when he unconsciously knows that he is rejected. 'Denial in phantasy and act' are perhaps the most common forms of defence in young children, as is 'undoing' whereby the forbidden impulse is negated by a form of negative magic. The individual may also try to make restitution for some real or phantasied misdemeanour.

One of the greatest problems caused by using defence mechanisms is the distortion of reality to which they give rise. This may impede the child's further emotional and cognitive development. If hating parents are seen as loving the child will be unable to respond to genuine affection without admitting that if the latter is love the former cannot be. Nor, indeed, will defences have the desired effect of reducing pain since the impulses and the objective pain will remain until they are brought under the conscious control of the ego and hence dealt with in a realistic manner.

Learning how to cope

During the long period of immaturity the human infant and child is faced with many new situations in both the animate and inanimate environment. He must learn to adapt to these experiences and this process of adaptation involves, initially, the use of reflexes, or built-in response mechanisms, and instincts. However, new situations soon arise which cannot be dealt with by instinctive reflexes and then the young human must try to cope. If these efforts are successful and he develops effective coping strategies he will achieve mastery in certain areas which will foster his 'competence orientation'.

At the start of her book *Children's Minds* Margaret Donaldson asked a question most pertinent to education today, when, speaking of schooling, she said: 'the problem then is to understand how something that begins so well can often end so badly. And inevitably, faced with this prolem, people turn to wondering whether schooling really does begin as well as it seems to do or whether the brightness of the early years carries within itself the shadow of the darkness that is to come' (p. 14). A partial answer is implied in the title of a BBC *Horizon* programme: 'If at first you don't succeed: you don't succeed.' Some children emerge from the vicissitudes of the first five years unable to cope with new environments or experiences and hence, irrespective of mental ability, are unable to develop their potential. Others have developed coping strategies and an orientation towards life which equip them to joyfully confront the challenges and disappointments awaiting them.

The relationship between 'defence' and 'coping' is not a simple one since, although sometimes a defensive reaction may be a useful way of coping with the situation, at other times defensiveness may impede the development of coping strategies. In general, attempts to maintain the *status quo* are seen as defensive whereas attempts either to adapt to the environment or to change it are seen as coping strategies. Murphy (1974) claimed that coping does not imply success but refers to the efforts a child makes to deal with 'threats and dangers, frustrations and defeats, obstacles, loss, strangeness and the new unknown demands from the adults and others in the environment' (p. 71). She and her research associates (1962), in a longitudinal study of the development of coping in a group of children in the American town of Topeka, have shown how the child's constitution, his family environment and his early experiences interact either to facilitate or inhibit his capacity to cope.

The children studied by Murphy had been observed by Escalone (1953) during their infancy, and it was found that infants who were able to shut out unwanted stimulation either by autonomous action or by protest were later more adept at coping with the environment. However, the ability to tolerate frustration in infancy was not helpful to the child, since it could result in apathy, unless it enabled the child to tolerate the normal amount of delay involved in reaching a goal. If the infant was successful in his attempts to control stimulation the authors suggested that he learnt that 'effort brings satisfaction'.

In general they found some sex differences relative to coping. Autonomous children seemed to be secure enough to ask for help when they needed it, but were not over-dependent. This was true of both boys and girls. However, the girls in the study showed a wider spread of autonomous behaviour than the boys since some of them were considerably more dependent than any of the boys. A correlation was found for girls, between their motor capacities, or physical prowess, and their coping capacity but no such correlation was found for the boys since there was too little variation in the boys' motor scores. Another general finding was the relationship between cognitive and emotional flexibility and ability to cope, although not all the children were equally flexible, or inflexible, in all areas.

Three of Murphy's case studies clearly illustrated the relationship between the child's temperament, family experiences and later coping style.

1 Initially Vernon was characterised by observing alertly, having considerable motor skill and being low in affective expression. He became watchful and constrained in new situations especially when dealing with adults. The authors commented, 'no boy showed more reserve or showed less gratification from his encounters with the environment than Vernon, despite his great competence, fine motor co-ordination, and capacity to manipulate objects' (1962, p. 328).

It appeared that his mother had been disappointed when he was born as he was a third boy and found his reserved and sensitive attitude as an infant difficult as she was an efficient, vigorous, outgoing woman. Nevertheless he was popular with his peers and more extravert in their company. It seemes that, despite some tension between Vernon and his mother, his development was fairly straightforward in that he made use of his alertness and motor skills while increasing his innate caution.

2 In Patsy's case her treatment as a baby deprived her of experiences which she particularly needed. As an infant Patsy most enjoyed physical

closeness and boisterous physical handling by her father. Her mother suffered from fatigue and only interacted with Patsy by smiling or speaking to her from a distance. She seldom touched her. Patsy seemed to respond to this by becoming a child who at the age of four kept her distance and appeared isolated and shy. The authors remarked that 'this solution was only partially satisfactory, and Patsy remained one of the children who "liked to hang around Mommy" into her school years beyond the time when most children were roaming autonomously over a wide territory. In other words, her unsatisfying solution of a basic and deep need led to a hierarchy of coping patterns, defensive in character, thus keeping her from the flexibility in development shown by other children whose coping styles reflected their natural inclinations'. (p. 330).

3 Daryl was a premature baby who was ill for a long period. Her mother saw her as pretty and fragile and spent most of her time dressing her up and hovering over her. Daryl clung to her mother and showed considerable hostility toward her younger siblings, with the exception of a younger sister whom she treated as her mother treated her. It seemed that provided she was appreciated for her physical attractiveness and could mother younger children she would cope. Indeed she did this when starting school, and her teacher reported that she was 'the most popular child'. 'Her anxiety . . . seemed to be handled by narcissistic satisfaction in her own prettiness, and her abilities to either shut out, control or elicit positive responses from others. We may say that she has used dependence as a major coping device, in which she could be relatively secure and free' (p. 331).

These three children all adapted to the situation in which they found themselves. However, certainly in Patsy's and Daryl's case, such adaptation, while satisfactory, did have a cost in terms of spontaneity and exuberance.

As a result of their study, Murphy and her co-workers found that the children were more likely to outgrow their earlier vulnerabilities than they had expected. In particular success at one stage led to even greater success at the next, together with enhanced self-esteem. It appeared that 'the struggle toward mastery has a motivating force of its own (p. 389). As the child learnt to deal with the environment in his own particular way so his sense of personal identity developed and was strengthened. The children who coped least well were those who repressed negative, hostile and anxious feelings. The overall findings of Murphy were summarised in a list of coping styles.

1 Children of low sensory sensitivity, low autonomic reactivity, low drive, and good developmental balance will function smoothly and naturally with moderate encounters with the environment, ease of control, mild gratification, and little compulsion to obtain more intense or a wider range of satisfaction. Their ease both of gratification and of control will help them to avoid guilt and hostility-arousing conflict with the environment.

2 By contrast, children of high sensitivity, high drive, autonomic reactivity, and good developmental balance will make active, vivid, quick contact with opportunities, maximize their use of them with a wider range of coping techniques, and show evidence of a high level of gratification. But their high drive will lead to more conflictual encounters with the environment. Other things being equal, the flexibility and adaptive resources implied in their good balance will help them to solve the problems resulting from these conflicts, with a resulting frustration-gratification balance on the positive side. But the greater tendency to get into conflict with the environment is apt to lead to a more complex emotional life, more fantasy.

3 When high sensitivity and high drive are accompanied by developmental imbalance, the danger of unpleasant sequelae of encounters with the environment will be greater. If the high drive precludes a capacity for delay, a child may deal with these possibilities by cautious or slow entrance into new situations, a tendency to be selective and to maintain safety within a narrow range. But gratification will be pursued energetically within this range and be intense when difficulties are mastered.

4 When high sensitivity is combined with high autonomic reactivity (especially with slow recovery), and with high drive but marked developmental imbalance involving deficiency, especially in the adaptive areas, the child will have great coping difficulties; he may have difficulty in the use of delay, selection, and other ways of controlling the impact of the environment, and be prone to disappointment except when he finds exactly the right scope for his areas of good equipment. (pp. 340-1)

The role of play in learning to cope

Through the activity of 'play' the child learns both about, and how to cope with, the physical environment and his social world. Play is enjoyable. It is also behaviour which is not real and is understood to be nonliteral by the participants. Thus those taking part are 'buffered' (Bruner,

1972) from the normal effects of their activities. Play thus simulates other behaviour, and allows the child to learn by trial and error in an environment which is comparatively safe both physically and psychologically. In addition to learning the child is able to work through feelings towards himself and others without the accompanying actions having the consequences that would follow if they were 'real' and not 'playful'. Here the feelings are indeed real but their manifestations are within the convention of play and are therefore acceptable both to the child and others.

Many years ago Wickes (1927) drew attention to the role of imaginary companions within the life of the young child. On the basis of her clinical experience she maintained that 'imaginary companions are called into existence because of a psychological need' (p. 157). For example, one child had a 'Mrs Comphret' as a companion, who personified all the qualities the child wished for, but had not found, in her own mother. Happy children who lacked peers used imaginary companions as playmates, and often children used them to act as projected parts of themselves, who could perform the actions which were normally prohibited. One particular child was so withdrawn, or introverted, that the fantasied other self was believed to exist within her. She told Wickes that 'I am larger than most girls of my age. I love beauty. I especially admire small girls with golden curls and deep blue eyes. I like to dream that there is such a person inside me, and that I am just a shell, and that some day all this outer appearance of me will drop off and I shall appear like the lovely princess in fairy tales, ravishingly beautiful, and lovable and gracious' (pp. 161-2).

Although imaginary companions can help the child to cope with internal and external conflicts, if the child's life becomes dominated by them they may have difficulty coming to terms with real life and real people. In general Wickes saw the process of individuation as requiring the child to try on many selves, and in this endeavour imaginary companions could be helpful since they could represent the 'ideal self or what the child would like to be or aspects of himself which the child repudiates' (p. 190).

Garvey (1977) argued that private fantasy and solitary play were 'secondary derived ways of playing'. To her social play was primary. Nor did she entirely accept Piaget's view of play which related it to developmental changes in cognition. For him (1951) play had three stages. Firstly, during the sensori-motor period, it was essentially concerned with action, the development of motor skills, and causing the reoccurrence of events. In the second stage (2-6 years), symbolic play occurred and the child began to pretend. Here he became able to relate the outside world to himself but did not attempt to relate himself to the outside world. In the third stage, which corresponded with school entry, the child began to co-operate with others and to compete with them in games which had rules and procedures. The child's understanding of rules was also seen to change. Initially they were regarded as absolute but later the child would realise that he and his peers could agree to change them in order to make the game more satisfactory for all.

Garvey (1977) based her studies on the observation of pairs of children, of similar ages (2-5 years), interacting when they were alone in the experimental play room. Her children all knew their partners prior to the experimental sessions. Their teachers commented that the children showed more social skills in the sessions than they did in their nursery school. Garvey argued that this could be because there were less distractions in the experimental setting, and therefore a child may have to 'learn to interact with more than one person at a time and acquire techniques for dealing with persons whose speech and conversational habits are not well known' (p. 20). This observation would support Bower's hypothesis (see p. 87) than an infant's apparent fear of strangers may be because the stranger cannot communicate with him as his mother does, and he has not learnt how to cope with this.

Of particular interest was Garvey's finding that by the age of three children were able to signal to each other whether or not the interaction they were engaged in was 'playing' or 'real' – a skill they could have learnt by distinguishing playful interactions with their parents and other adults from reality-oriented ones. In addition, the content of the children's play was seen to change as they matured. She therefore believed that

> the study of spontaneous play can provide a rich source of information about the nature of a child's competence. Children at play enact or represent knowledge of their social and material world they cannot verbalise explicitly, or demonstrate in the setting of experimental tasks. (p. 118)

Summary

During the course of the separation-individuation process the child will have experiences with children and adults which increase his feelings of self-adequacy, and self-esteem, or his view of himself as valuable and worthwhile despite his limited abilities and skills. Coopersmith, in his study *The Antecedents of Self-Esteem* (1967), demonstrated that parents who were emotionally stable had children who were high in self-esteem. Children with demanding and critical parents were not only low in self-esteem but were also depressed and pessimistic: 'the corrosive drizzle of negative appraisal presumably removes the joy of today and the anticipation of tomorrow' (p. 130). Children with low self-esteem and their parents seemed to be most concerned with pleasing others. They also judged themselves by the evaluations of others rather than unconcernedly pursuing their own activities and goals. That is, the child's degree of autonomous functioning was related to his feelings of self-esteem.

The process of learning to cope is a lengthy one, beginning as it does in the first year of life and continuing throughout the pre-school period – nor is it completed then. Nevertheless, by the time the child enters school he will have developed a series of coping strategies and will tend either to 'cope' or to 'defend' when faced with new challenges. This tendency will influence his behaviour and will facilitate or inhibit his further development. Indeed Coleman (1966) found that a child's self-concept and feeling of being in control of events affected his performance during the later years of school more than did his family background or the type of school he attended. If a child cannot begin to cope with learning because his previous experiences have inhibited his curiosity, stifled his individuality and lowered his self-esteem, then changes in teaching methods or in the curriculum will be ineffective until his belief in himself is restored and his autonomy developed. The secure, independent, hopeful child will learn better in some environments than others but the insecure, defensive child is too engaged with his internal conflicts to benefit, more than marginally, from an, apparently, facilitating environment.

6

The child in the family: influences on learning

Introduction

We have now reached the point where the developmental strands described in the previous chapters must be drawn together to show their influence on the child's ability to learn. By the age of two or three the child becomes aware that he is a member of a family group consisting of himself, his mother, his father and, often, his siblings. In addition, his interaction with the world outside the family will begin to be extended and will culminate with his entry into school. At this moment the familiar environment of the home will be replaced by one which, even if stimulating and exciting, will be, essentially, strange. At home learning has been, mainly, unintentional; at school, although unintentional learning will continue, the child will be expected to conform to certain standards of behaviour and will be required to learn, intentionally, skills such as reading and writing, and to develop basic notions of numeracy. In this task he will be surrounded by other children, of whose appraisals he will be aware, and expected to interact with a strange adult, his 'teacher', for several hours each day. The only equipment which the child has to deal with this situation is his repertoire of coping strategies, his belief and expectations. Unlike the new-born infant, biological predispositions will be a very minor factor for the five-year-old. His sensori-motor intelligence will have been replaced by pre-operational thinking (see p. 114), and although this will be broadly similar for all children there will be more diversity between them than would have been the case three years earlier. Nevertheless, similarity is probably still more apparent than difference in that children's thinking at age five is more like that of each other than it is like that of the adults with whom they interact. Nor does it show the variation apparent in the intellectual functioning of these same adults. However, the children's communicative competence will be beginning to exhibit observable differences. The greatest variation will be in how the children feel about themselves and others and hence respond to the challenge of entering school.

The oedipal period

Although the child has been aware of his father as a significant adult since infancy, it is only during the pre-school and early school years (approximately 2-6 years) that the child seems to be affected by realising the special relationship between the mother and father, by becoming aware that they are different sexes and, by developing a personal sexual identity. The young child therefore has to deal with a triangular relationship between himself and the two most significant adults in his life within the context of early sexual awareness. At this stage two further factors are of importance: firstly, the child lives an emotional life the intensity of which is apparent to any person who observes young children, and, secondly, his cognitive development has only reached the stage called 'pre-operational' by Piaget. This stage is characteristically one in which things are as they seem to be rather than as they, logically, must be. For example, if a child is shown two balls of plasticine and agrees that they contain the same amount of plasticine, and if one ball is then rolled out into a sausage shape, the child will say that the sausage now contains more, or less, plasticine. He does not realise that if nothing is added and nothing taken away, regardless of appearance, the amount remains the same. Additionally, the child's own view of the world is believed by him to be an accurate representation of reality. He has difficulty understanding that while he has one point of view another person may have another, and adapting his thinking to take this into account. Finally, the child, although able to observe changes in both the animate and inanimate environment, explains these changes in a way which is foreign to the adult mind. Piaget (1930) asked children questions concerning natural phenomena (e.g. 'why do clouds move?') and found that before the age of six or seven physical explanations were seldom given, rather the child believed that objects had motives or could be affected, in a magical way, by human wishes, including his own.

The pre-school child thus inhabits an intuitive cognitive world, dominated by magically induced changes and centred upon his own perceptions of situations and events. He is beset by intense feelings and has to come to terms with the emotional and intellectual puzzles which arise when he considers his parents' relationship to each other and to him in a context of observable sexual differences. This period, with its attendant developmental hurdles, was called by Freud (1897, 1910) the period of the 'oedipus complex'. This nomenclature has given rise to some basic misunderstandings and misleading half truths, since it implies that the boy wishes to have sexual intercourse with his mother and murder his father. Sophocles' play *Oedipus Rex* is based on adult sexuality, and explores the realities of adult political life, the inherent danger of adult self-knowledge, and the fragility of human happiness. None of these notions are directly relevant to the development of the pre-school child's sexual identification, preceding his seeking a heterosexual love object at puberty.

During the oedipal period Freud argued that the boy must give up his initial choice of his mother as a love object, establish a secure identification with his father, and thus be free to make heterosexual relationships in the future. This developmental sequence was thought to start when the boy realises that while he and other males have a penis females do not. Thus he gets the idea that a penis can be absent. Freud's belief was that the boy fears that his penis will be cut off. As Dolto (1936) pointed out, masturbation is usually prohibited by parents, as are other activities with libidinal content, such as aggressiveness in boys and flirtatiousness in girls, curiosity and exploration. The child thus gets pleasure from his penis but this is accompanied by guilt and fear. At the same time he feels love for his mother, in the sense of wanting to be with her to the exclusion of others. However his father is clearly closely attached to his mother, and she to him, and hence he views his father as a rival. Since he feels hostility to his father he believes that his father feels hostility to him. He fears that his father will castrate him as a punishment for his wish to obtain sole possession of the mother. In addition he loves his father, as he has done since infancy, and feels concerned that his murderous impulses will damage him. (Given the magical thinking characteristic of the pre-operational child such a sequence of feelings and fears is indeed possible.) Thus just as the infant in the first year felt ambivalent towards the frustrating and loving mother, so the oedipal boy feels ambivalent towards the father of whom and for whom he has fear. He sees him as a rival and yet the father is a male like himself and possesses many qualities which he would like to possess. It is out of the conflict caused by identification with the father together with love for the mother that the boy's oedipus complex develops.

A little boy will exhibit a special interest in his father; he would like to grow like him, and be like him and take his place everywhere ... he takes his father as an ideal ... At the same time as the identification with his father, or a little later, the boy has begun to develop a true object cathexis towards his mother according to the attachment (anaclitic) type. He then exhibits, therefore, two psychologically distinct ties: a straightforward sexual object – cathexis towards his mother and an identification with his father which takes him as his model. The two subsist side by side for a time without any mutual influence or interference. In consequence of the irresistable advance towards a unification of mental life, they come together at last; and the normal oedipus complex originates from their confluence. The little boy notices that his father stands in his way with his mother. His identification with his father then takes on a hostile colouring and becomes identical with the wish to replace his father in regard to his mother as well. Identification, in fact, is ambivalent from the very first; it can turn into an expression of tenderness as easily as into a wish for someone's removal.' (Freud, 1921)

Since 'childish love has no bounds but also no aim, it is doomed to disappointment' (Freud, 1932), the oedipus complex will, in normal circumstances be resolved when the child applies the reality principle to the situation, thus freeing his libidinal energy for intellectual and cultural exploration during the latency period. If it is not resolved the child will not turn from his parents to his peers and school work and there may well be difficulties outside the home stemming from the unresolved conflicts inside it. However, in order for the child to apply the reality principle he needs the help of his parents as representatives of the reality which he must accept. Firstly, he needs to be aware that his father is, indeed, the prime object of his mother's love. If she, through disappointment in her marital relationships, unconsciously seeks for substitute satisfactions through her son, then he will, as it were, continue to live in hope. Secondly, if the father reacts to his son's rivalry with punitiveness then the son will indeed identify with him but it will be identification based on fear (as expressed in the slogan 'If you can't beat 'em: join 'em') or what Anna Freud (1937) called 'Identification with the aggressor'. This will lead him to seek to please or placate the father and thus inhibit his subsequent independent development.

A further complication that is often left out of accounts of the oedipus complex is the inherent bisexuality of both children and adults. As early as 1899 Freud commented in a letter to Fliess that he was beginning to see the sexual act as one in which 'four persons are involved' (p. 289). In

The Ego and the Id (1923) he argued that the boy also has a feminine attitude towards the father, springing from his feminine aspect, and thus feels rivalry with the mother. 'It is this complicating element introduced by bisexuality that makes it so difficult to obtain a clear view of the facts in connection with the earliest object-choices and identifications, and still more to describe them intelligently'. Thus the boy will contain both masculine and feminine elements, and while a successful resolution of the oedipus complex will result in the masculine elements predominating the female ones should not be totally repressed, nor will they be if the father's own masculine and feminine elements are well integrated in his personality structure. However, if the boy adopts a feminine attitude as a counterbalance to his father's masculinity this will give rise to passive homosexual tendencies.

The boy's identification with the father, in addition to enabling him to identify with the same sex parent, accept the impossibility of exclusive maternal possession, and free libidinal energy, will also cause him to internalise both the image of the father as an ideal to be emulated and the father's rules and regulations concerning how the child ought to behave. Thus, in Freud's words, the superego is the 'heir to the oedipus complex' (1924). Therefore if the oedipus complex is not resolved satisfactorily the child's superego development will be affected. He will either have one which is too strict, and hence comes into conflict with the ego, or he will be deficient in internal controls thus prolonging into adult life the amoral approach to others characteristic of the pre-oedipal child.

Freud believed, initially, that the little girl's development was similar to that of the boy's but his clinical work soon made him realise that this was not so. However, throughout his life Freud had difficulty understanding female sexual development. In 1905 he said that women's sexual life was 'veiled in impenetrable obscurity' and wrote later that 'we know less about the sexual life of little girls than of boys. But we need not feel ashamed of this distinction; after all the sexual life of adult women is a "dark continent" for psychology' (Freud, 1926a). With reference to the oedipus complex his view was that when the girl realises that she has not got a penis she blames her mother for this and turns against her, the original love object. Thus the fantasied act of castration is the trigger which starts the girl's oedipal development, whereas it is the fear of castration which marks the beginning of the end of the boy's development. The girl, once she realises that she lacks a penis, develops a wish to have a child which will symbolically represent her penis, she therefore turns to her father hoping that he will give her the wished-for child. Now the girl must apply the same reality principle as the boy and realize that her mother is the prime object of her father's love. In the same way her complex will be resolved if she gives up her father and seeks an independent male love object, having first identified with her mother. Fear of castration cannot impede her from identifying with her mother; nevertheless, if she perceives her mother (and women in general) as occupying an oppressed position her difficulties become almost insuperable. She cannot be a man, although she may well envy the power and possibilities that possession of a penis seems to imply, nor does she wish to be identified with one whom she perceives as inferior. By applying the reality principle she may both 'know her place' and reject it. The nature of such a conflict was described by the adolescent Ursula in *The Rainbow*:

> Then gradually the heaviness of her heart pressed and pressed into consciousness. What was she doing? Was she bearing a child? Bearing a child? To what?
>
> Her flesh thrilled but her soul was sick. It seemed, this child, like the seal set on her own nullity. Yet she was glad in her flesh that she was with child . . . What did the self, the form of life matter? . . . Was it not enough that she had her man, her children, her place of shelter under the sun? Was it not enough for her, as it had been enough for her mother? (Lawrence, 1915, pp. 484-5)

Freud also believed that since the girl did not fear castration her motivation for super ego development was fear of loss of love and disappointment that her oedipal wishes could not be realized. Because of this motivation he thought that she would not develop as strong a super ego as the male. Jahoda (1977) also pointed out that while Freud, theoretically, attributed the same bisexuality to the female as he did to the male, in fact he did not do so. She quoted Freud's remark that analysis 'is most difficult when trying to persuade a woman to abandon her wish for a penis or convince a man that passive attitudes towards another man are sometimes indispensable' (Freud, 1937), and commented, 'note the asymmetry of formulation: men need to be persuaded of the legitimacy of psychological bisexuality while women have to abandon the idea of psychological bisexuality' (p. 87).

Whether or not the Freudian account is verifiable, it is clear that all infants have, initially, a close tie to their mothers and may well seek exclusive possession of her. By the time the child enters school this infantile dependence needs to have been dissolved so that he is free to explore the ever widening world as well as form friendships with peers. In addition the child will have realised that there are morphological and social differences between the sexes and will have adopted sex-typical behaviour to a greater or lesser degree. Identification with the same sex parent will facilitate the child's accommodation to sexual identity so that masculinity and femininity will be valued both in the self and others. Such an accommodation requires the child's prime gender identity to match his morphological sexual characteristics, i.e. a boy needs to accept that he is primarily masculine and a girl that she is primarily feminine. Once this crucial developmental stage has been reached the child can enter the emotionally less tempestuous period of latency and move, cognitively, into the period of 'concrete operations' with the confident expectation that he will be able to meet its challenges with joy since he knows who and what he is. This mood is caught by A.A. Milne's verse (1927):

> When I was One,
> I had just begun.
>
> When I was Two,
> I was nearly new.
>
> When I was Three,
> I was hardly Me.
>
> When I was Four,
> I was not much more
>
> When I was Five,
> I was just alive.
>
> But now I am Six, I'm as clever as clever.
> So I think I'll be six now for ever and ever.

Not until the resurgence of sexual feeling at puberty and the start of the final stage of cognitive development, that of 'formal operations' when the child will be able to think abstractly about both the physical and the social world, will the belief that he is 'as clever as clever' need to be stringently reassessed.

Siblings

Although during the first year, and to a lesser extent the second year, the primary influence on the infant is that of his parents, especially his mother, increasingly potent sources of influence are his siblings and

Table 6.1 *Combinations of ordinal position and sex of siblings in a two-child family* (Adapted from Sutton-Smith and Rosenberg, 1970)

Boy with younger brother	M1M
Boy with younger sister	M1F
Boy with older brother	MM2
Boy with older sister	FM2
Girl with younger brother	F1M
Girl with younger sister	F1F
Girl with older brother	MF2
Girl with older sister	FF2

Table 6.2 *Combinations of ordinal position and sex of siblings in a three-child family* (Adapted from Sutton-Smith and Rosenberg, 1970)

Male positions

Boy with two younger brothers	M1MM
Boy with a younger brother and below him a younger sister	M1MF
Boy with a younger sister and below her a younger brother	M1FM
Boy with two younger sisters	M1FF
Boy with an older and younger brother	MM2M
Boy with an older brother and younger sister	MM2F
Boy with an older sister and younger brother	FM2M
Boy with an older and younger sister	FM2F
Boy with two older brothers	MMM3
Boy with an older sister and above her an older brother	MFM3
Boy with an older brother and above him an older sister	FMM3
Boy with two older sisters	FFM3

Female positions

F1FF	F1MF	F1FM	F1MM
FF2F	FF2M	MF2F	MF2M
FFF3	FMF3	MFF3	MMF3

peers. Sibling influence has been studied and reviewed extensively by Sutton-Smith and Rosenberg (1970) who maintained that not only should the ordinal position of the child in the family be considered but also whether his siblings were of the same or the opposite sex. There are eight possible combinations in a two-child family (Table 6.1) and twenty-four in a three-child (Table 6.2). For convenience Sutton-Smith and Rosenberg devised a system of notation to express these relationships:

> The letter M refers to male; the letter F, to female. The order of sequence from left to right is the order of males and females in the family from oldest to youngest. The particular person we are referring to is the one with the number after his M or F; that number also represents his birth order in the family. (p. 17)

The effect that siblings had on a child was found to vary depending on the child's ordinal position and the sex of the siblings, and this combination was called 'sibling status'. Sutton-Smith and Rosenberg were most concerned with 'those conditions of learning that have created the effects regularly associated with sibling status' (p. 13). Within a social learning framework they used the concepts of 'operant learning' (i.e. learning to repeat an initially random form of behaviour because it is positively reinforced), 'modeling' and 'interaction'.

Children were found to be affected by the sex of their siblings especially in two-child families in a number of ways. In general children with opposite sex siblings had less social interaction within their families but heightened self-concern. When there was an age gap of two to four years between the children Koch (1956) showed that six-year-olds experienced opposite sex siblings as both more stimulating and more stressful; this effect was most noticeable in the first-borns. Opposite sex siblings also affected a child's sex-typical behaviour. In particular a boy with a sister was more feminine than boys with other sibling combinations, whereas a boy with two sisters was more masculine, possibly suggesting some form of counteraction to their influence. Girls with brothers had a particularly stable sexual identification. There was also some evidence that in two-child families an opposite sex sibling would intensify traits normally associated with one sex in the sibling of the other. Thus in FM2 and MF2 families the boy in the first combination was more affiliative and the girl in the second more achieving. It was suggested that, because of the first-born's greater power, the second child modelled itself on the first and hence developed opposite-sex traits. There are however changes with age; the boys in the FM2 family appeared withdrawn and depressed at six while their sisters were outgoing and enthusiastic, whereas at ten the girls had become submissive and the boys slightly above average in domineering behaviour. They were also found to be the most powerful of all the second-borns in terms of influencing the behaviour of their older sibling.

It was shown that on many measures first-born girls are similar to second-born boys, and first-born boys to second-born girls. The former appeared to be more 'feminine', 'tender-minded' and conforming, the latter were 'masculine' and 'tough minded' and non-conforming. It was also found (Schooler and Caudill, 1964) that first-born males and second-born females had higher rates of admission to psychiatric hospitals. The reasons for this are not clear. While it is true that the traits associated with the M1F/MF2 combination are not sex typical for the boys they should not affect the females adversely. However Sutton-Smith and Rosenberg point out that if to be first-born implies being closer to the parents and being expected to carry out some parental duties, whereas the second born is expected to be more autonomous, this would, once again, be sexually inappropriate for the first-born boy and for the second-born girl. Similarly, Rothbart's (1967) findings that mothers were tougher with their first-born daughters and second-born sons and more tender and praising towards their first-born sons and second-born daughters, would facilitate more sex-appropriate behaviour in the first group especially with respect to the boys.

Later born children, as a group, appeared to be more aggressive than first-borns or, at least, expressed their aggression more openly, unlike the first-borns who, because of their greater adult identification, were found by Koch (1955) to be more adult in their expressions of hostility, especially in their use of verbal criticism. First-borns were also seen to be more like adults in their behaviour, thus suggesting that they model themselves on adults as well as responding to their influence, whereas later borns were more likely to model themselves on older siblings and were less exposed to adult influence since their older siblings deflect it to a certain extent. First-born children, unlike later borns, have had the disconcerting experience of being displaced from their position of being the sole recipient of parental care. A study by Gewirtz (1948) neatly demonstrated the effect of this displacement. He was interested in 'succorance seeking behaviour', or asking for help and reassurance. He divided succorance seeking into three forms: (1) directly seeking help; (2) indirectly seeking succorance by asking for reassurance or requiring body contact; and (3) hostile attention seeking, i.e. getting attention by behaving in an aggressive manner suggesting that the child wished for reassurance but, fearing that it would not be forthcoming, showed conflict concerning the expression of his need. When he observed four- and five-year-old children he found that only children and the youngest children in a family directly sought help, first-borns sought it indirectly and were the least aggressive of the children, and middle-born children showed most negative attention-getting behaviour. Sutton-Smith and Rosenberg summarise the findings by saying,

> ... only children (and younger born) will tend to show an uncontaminated expectation of help from others; they will, therefore, use affiliation as an instrumental behaviour. But first-borns, having suffered a mild defeat for the same expectations, will seek more reassurance and comfort, so that they come to use affiliation as a consummatory behaviour or end state (in itself). And again middle-born will show an aggressiveness toward getting attention, rejecting affiliation as a means of behaviour. (1970, p. 98)

In connection with cognitive development Koch (1954) demonstrated that, when there was a two- to four-year age gap between the children, children with brothers were superior to children with sisters on tests of verbal meaning or quantitative tests. Similar effects were found by Schoonover (1959) and Altus (1962). But Rosenberg and Sutton-Smith (1964; 1966) found the reverse, i.e. female subjects who had female siblings did better than those who had male siblings, except in three-child families when the presence of males helped second- and third-born girls. It appeared that the age difference between the children was particularly important, in that when there was a two- to three-year gap girls with girl siblings showed increased performance whereas boy pairs showed decreased performance. The authors suggested that for a girl to be dependent on a sibling who is close in age is sexually appropriate and facilitates their learning, whereas boys were adversely affected by feelings of rivalry and competition. However no such effects appeared when there was only one year between the children.

In any social group there will be attempts by the members to influence each other, and the family is no exception. Commonsense would suggest, and research has confirmed, that only children perceive parents as being more powerful, relative to themselves, than do children with siblings. In addition children more readily understand and accept discipline from other children since, 'adults judge child behaviour by adult standards; children judge it by child standards. This means that discipline imposed by children on each other will seem more reasonable and have more meaning' (Bossard and Boll, 1960, pp. 154-5). Only children will thus feel more oppressed and powerless than others. First-borns appear to look two ways, as they see parents as more powerful than themselves but also see themselves as in a dominant position with respect to their younger siblings. Later born children experience two types of power over them: the power of the parents and the power of their older siblings who, while being more powerful, are also more like themselves. This led Sutton-Smith and Rosenberg to hypothesise that in later life first-borns would be more at ease in hierarchical situations, where they could be submissive to those above them and dominate those below, whereas later borns would be more egalitarian. Exner in a personal communication to them of his study of Peace Corps Volunteers supported their hypothesis since first-borns were more successful in the hierarchically structured societies of Eastern Asia and later borns in more open-ended situations, such as obtain in Micronesia. Later borns also appeared to be more popular with their peers since they were less inclined to dominate them and were more egalitarian in approach (Schachter, 1964; Finneran, 1958). Sutton-Smith and Rosenberg studied in great detail the way in which siblings influenced one another by asking children both how their siblings got them to do what they wanted and how they got their siblings to conform to their own wishes. Generally first-borns were more 'bossy' whereas second-borns nagged, were 'bothersome' and appealed to their parents for help. In one study (1966) they asked girls to role play the 'bossy' and 'bothersome' role and asked a group of judges to rate the children on their performance in both roles and to say which role they identified with. What they found was that second-borns were better at role playing in general, perhaps reflecting their greater role diffusion, but also that the raters identified with the 'bossy' or 'bothersome' role depending on whether they themselves were first-borns or later borns, with the first-borns identifying with the 'bossy' role and vice versa. This seemed to imply that 'adult preference for others was to a considerable extent consistent with enduring sibling-association influences throughout the growth years' (1970, p. 58). Later borns were found to show more empathy with people whom they saw as similar to themselves and with whom they could interact (Stotland and Dunn, 1962, 1963), which Stotland interpreted as being similar to their experience of living with older siblings.

Siblings effects, however, are not static and there seems to be some consistent changes over age. For example, Sutton-Smith and Rosenberg found that when they looked at MM2 children these boys were the most masculine, least feminine and least anxious of all. However, between nine and thirteen years there was a great increase in dependency, which coincided with their brother's transfer to secondary school. At sixteen they, once again, showed a great increase in dominance and independence so that their profiles were similar to those obtained between the ages of six and nine. In sex role development they argued that children learn 'structurally different repertoires over the years' and that the boys' development differs from the girls'. Thus from 0-5 years boys and girls learn the 'affective-humanistic' repertoire from their mothers; from 5-15 boys develop the 'athletic-aggressive' repertoire and girls the 'nurturant domestic one' from peers; and after 15 boys the 'entrepreneurial-managerial' and girls the 'feminine-glamour' from teachers. There is however considerable individual variation.

Only children were found to differ from others in that they showed more dependency and achievement motivation together with high self-esteem. They were also likely to identify closely with the opposite sex parent and the boys tended to be more feminine than the norm and girls more masculine. Mothers were found to be much more nurturant to only boys than to only girls (Cushna, 1966). Cryan (1968) looked at the femininity scores of fathers, mothers and daughters in only-girl families and found the fathers scores varied with their daughters whereas the mothers varied but in the opposite direction. Adjustment in these families seemed to involve a masculine father and daughter and a highly feminine mother. All only children do seem to suffer from undue adult influence. As Bossard and Boll (1960) argued,

> Life among siblings is like living in the nude, psychologically speaking. Siblings serve as a constant rude awakening. On the other hand, siblings save each other from being with their parents and adults too much. The significance of this is that they are kept from the unnatural environment, which the adult furnishes. (p. 91)

Learning how to learn

Up to the age of approximately five years the child will learn, but such learning is unintentional or incidental. During his formal education there will be an intentional attempt to teach him certain skills thought necessary for adult life. He will, however, continue to learn incidentally by observation and modelling. The manner in which a child copes with intentional attempts to teach him by parents, teachers and others is influenced by his self-esteem, his coping strategies and his understanding of the learning situation. Where one child will expect success another will merely be motivated to defend himself against failure, and a third will withdraw from a situation which he has come to see as totally confusing, much as the infants studied by the Papoušeks (1977) withdrew when the tasks became too complex for them.

Baumrind (1967) was concerned with the development of 'instrumental competence' which was defined by 'social responsibility' (that is, a friendly attitude to peers in contrast with a hostile one leading to disruptive behaviour), 'independence', 'achievement orientation' and 'vitality'. She carried out a series of studies to see how a child's instrumental competence was affected by his previous interactions with parents and other socialising adults. In her first study she was able to divide four-year-olds into three groups:

1 Those ranked as 'mature': that is, who were friendly towards their peers and had high achievement orientation, vitality and independence.
2 Those who were particularly poor at interacting with peers, low on vitality, and not rated highly on the other measures.
3 The 'immature', who were characterised by low self-reliance and self-control.

The 'mature' children had parents who exercised 'authoritative' parent control, i.e. they were comparatively controlling but offered a considerable amount of warmth and positive encouragement. These parents gave clear instructions to their children, and relied on corporal punishment rather than withdrawal of love, ridicule or fear. The second group of children had 'authoritarian' parents who were detached, non-nurturant and controlling. They used coercive methods rather than rational ones and were the most likely, of all the parents, to justify their demands for obedience by appealing to religious beliefs or the need to show respect for parents. The parents of the 'immature' children were labelled 'permissive'. These parents were warmer than those who were authoritarian but less warm than were the authoritative parents. They made few demands on their children and did not feel that they were in control of their children's behaviour. The attempts at control that were made were backed by threats of withdrawal of love or ridicule. A second longitudinal study separated the children by sex, but the results were the same.

Baumrind's studies suggested that warmth, control and an organized environment were significantly related to the development of instrumental competence in children. Studies of mothers acting as teachers to their young child point in a similar direction. One of the earliest and best known series of studies on this topic are those of Hess and Shipman (1965, 1967). In their first study they presented three arguments:

1 The behaviour that leads to societal, educational and economic poverty is socialised in early childhood.
2 The central quality involved in the effects of cultural deprivation is a lack of cognitive meaning in the mother-child communication system.
3 The growth of cognitive processes is fostered in family control systems which offer and permit a wide range of alternatives of action and thought and that such growth is constricted by systems of control which offer predetermined solutions and few alternatives for consideration and choice (p. 870).

They believed that the basic problem was the process by which 'cultural experience is translated into cognitive behaviour and academic achievement' (p. 870). They therefore decided to study the way mothers both communicate and interact with their children in a reactive situation and in particular to observe, firstly, whether the child's behaviour was impulsive or reflective and, secondly, whether they had an outgoing active approach to learning or a passive compliant one.

They studied 140 black mothers and their four-year-old children who were selected from four social classes: (1) professional executive and managerial; (2) skilled blue collar; (3) unskilled or semi-skilled; (4) unskilled or semi-skilled, but with fathers absent. The experimental design was for the mothers to be taught three tasks: (1) to sort out a group of plastic toys in terms of their colour and function; (2) to divide up eight blocks using two characteristics simultaneously; (3) to copy five designs using Etch-a-Sketch. They were then asked to teach these tasks to their children. Hess and Shipman found that the group 1 mothers were much more likely to explain the task clearly to the child at the outset and to speak more to the child. All mothers showed affection for their children but the lower-class mothers were not able to structure the situation in a way that made it meaningful for the child. The authors then argued that mothers who interacted with their children in such a way that the children saw the environment as coherent, patterned and meaningful would be more likely to succeed in formal learning situations.

Brophy (1970) continued this early work by looking at the way in which the mothers gave meaning to specific pieces of child behaviour, in particular how the mothers gave their children relevant pieces of information when teaching them the Hess and Shipman tasks. He found that the middle-class mothers gave specific information before the child started on

Table 6.3 *Mean frequency of mother's use of positive v. negative reinforcement*
(From Feschbach, 1973)

	Middle-class white	Middle-class black	Lower-class white	Lower-class black
Positive reinforcement	6.5	4.7	4.7	4.8
Negative reinforcement	1.4	2.0	2.2	5.4

the task whereas the working-class mothers were more likely to correct him once he had made a mistake.

Feschbach (1973) pursued a related line of enquiry by concentrating on the amount of positive versus negative reinforcement received by the child from the mother in a learning situation. Firstly she studied four groups of mother-child pairs (middle-class white; middle-class black; lower-class white; lower-class black) and checked the amount of positive versus negative reinforcement given by the mothers when they were teaching puzzles to their four-year-olds. The results (Table 6.3) showed that the middle-class white child received the most positive reinforcement together with the least negative, whereas the lower-class black child, while receiving average amounts of positive reinforcement, received considerably more negative reinforcement than all the other children. Feschbach then looked at the relationship between the mother's behaviour and the child's success in learning to read. For this study she selected a group of forty 'comfortably off' middle-class mothers who had children who were either good or problem readers together with eighty other sixth-grade good or problem readers. She then observed the mothers interacting with their own child, one good, and one poor, reader whilst the child was engaged on a series of cognitive tasks. She found that while the amount of positive reinforcement given was the same for all mothers, the mothers of the problem readers used considerably more negative reinforcement both with their own and other children, including the good readers. They also used many more directive and controlling statements. Feschbach concluded that the way a child is taught may be as important as what he is taught. Another important question is why negative reinforcement is so counterproductive. Possibly it is symptomatic of a more general tension in the mother-child relationship, arguably springing from unconscious hostility on both sides.

A child's sex and position in the family will affect the type of learning experience to which he is exposed. In general boys appear to be more cognitively affected by their emotional tie to their mothers and hence her influence is more enduring for them (Yarrow, 1964). Sutton-Smith and Rosenberg (1970) found first-born males to be more verbal than second-born males but found no such effect for females. First-born children have been shown in many studies to be higher in their need for achievement and to be over-represented in higher education and in lists of eminent people. Although these findings have been challenged, if they are true one possible reason could be that first-borns identify more closely with their parents than do later borns and may therefore be more likely to value activities, such as school achievement, which are also valued by adults. Several studies have shown that mothers do treat their first-borns differently and this may be a partial explanation for the greater achievement of the first-borns, especially the first-born males. Hilton (1967) observed that when children were solving puzzles mothers of first-born and only children were much more interfering, inconsistent, likely to give task-oriented suggestions and give love for success while withholding love for failure than were the mothers of later born children. Rothbart (1967) found almost identical effects and pointed to the mothers' greater pressure for achievement on the first-borns. Mothers were also seen to have much higher expectations for their first-borns than for later borns (Cushna, 1966) and to be more directive (Stout, 1960). Sutton-Smith and Rosenberg (1970) summarise the first-borns' dilemma by saying that the parents

> expect more from them and treat them in an inconsistent manner. The first-born's continuing need for reassurance and guidance appears to evoke contradictory behaviour from the parents. The child seeks help but performs well. The parent gives help but is critically expectant of an even higher level of performance. Each member in this uneven synchrony is calibrated to the other. (p. 107)

Younger children seem to receive much less pressure and, at times, to be relatively neglected. This is particularly true of middle children. Bossard (1945) demonstrated, by transcribing conversations at the meal table, that the parents geared their talk to the intellectual level of the eldest child and paid less attention to requests for word meaning from the younger children. In learning terms first-borns are more likely to be using operant learning and later borns to be modelling their behaviour on older siblings, or using observational learning.

The above studies concentrate on maternal behaviour. Of equal importance is the extent to which a child believes that he himself, rather than
others, is responsible for his academic success or failure. Crandall,
Katkovsky and Crandall (1965) devised an 'Intellectual Achievement
Responsibility' (IAR) questionnaire to test the strength of this belief in
children. This was followed by McGhee and Crandall's (1968) finding a
relationship, particularly for girls, between belief in self-responsibility and
academic success. The boys only attributed to themselves responsibility
for their failures. Katkovsky et al. (1967) related parental behaviour to a
child's belief in internal versus external control in an achievement situation. They, too, found a sex difference. In general fathers' attitudes
seemed to affect boys and girls more than mothers' attitudes, but nurturant mothers had sons who were more likely to accept responsibility,
especially for failure. For girls, a belief in external control seemed to occur
when the mothers were rejecting or dominant.

Although there have been a number of studies, reviewed by Radin
(1976), of the effect of fathers on their children's cognitive development
the findings seem to present 'an array of contradictory and overlapping
evidence' (p. 268). However, Radin did claim that

> several trends, varying in strength, can be detected. Paternal nurtur-
> ance appears to be closely associated with the cognitive competence of
> boys, but not girls. A close relationship between father and son seems
> to foster an analytic cognitive style in the child. There are indications
> that powerful fathers foster their sons' cognitive development,
> provided the power is not used to intimidate the boys while they are
> engaged on mastery efforts. As to girls, some degree of autonomy and
> distance from fathers appears to be associated with cognitive profici-
> ency, although specific father interest in his daughter's academic
> progress appears to stimulate her intellectual growth. For both males
> and females authoritarian paternal behaviour tends to be associated
> with reduced academic competence, as does intense paternal involve-
> ment in problem-solving activities of the child. (p. 269)

Generally studies of learning how to learn suggest that children develop a
positive attitude to learning if the parents are warm, concerned, and orga-
nised; but not when they are interfering, overconcerned and cold. The
significance of these findings is that even before a child arrives at school he
may have developed an orientation towards the task of learning, which
will affect his initial interactions with teachers. These initial encounters
may set the tone for subsequent ones, thus supporting the hypothesis that

success breeds success and failure breeds failure. The slow cognitive decline of many children during their school lives may well be attributable, in part, to the nature of their school experience but it is also arguable that the potential for failure was present prior to their entering school. It is the interaction of their initial expectations with their school experience which actualises this potential. The converse, of course, should also be born in mind, i.e. that failure is not inevitable. If the school can compensate for the child's earlier setbacks then he may well overcome them. However, before this can be done it is essential to understand the nature of these developmental conflicts.

Conclusion

The clinical, experimental and observational findings reviewed suggest that, as the young human moves from dependence to independence, he develops an orientation towards the world which will affect his feelings of being able to cope, and this feeling will, in turn, affect his approach to new cognitive challenges. This is because the infant adapts to the environment as he experiences it and develops both coping strategies and defence mechanisms which determine his future competence. How then does this come about? Broadly, three stages can be discerned: (1) dependent infancy; (2) the separation-individuation period; and (3) from toddlerhood to school entry. In each of these stages the infant is faced with particular developmental challenges. The first gives him his sense of efficacy and his understanding of environmental consistency. In the second, coping strategies and defence mechanisms appear together with the start of autonomous functioning. In the third stage the child begins to see himself as a member of a family and starts to engage in intentional learning with a greater, or lesser, sense of competence.

The findings discussed support the notion that the child's ability to cope and become competent is related to his having experienced a comprehensible, intimate environment. The young child also needs to explore the world of objects and the social world outside the home. Although his thinking differs from that of adults he needs to interact with them while developing his ability to communicate, his autonomy, and his identity. In addition the child is learning to live in a family with the problems and possibilities inherent in his understanding of both his triangular relationship with his parents and his, qualitatively, different relationships with his siblings when they exist. These discrete experiences result in learning and adaptation. Since it is not possible for the child to benefit from alternative experiences which he has not had, his behaviour is shaped by what he believes a situation to be. This present belief depends on his understanding of, and cognitive and affective adaptation to, previously occurring situations. It appears therefore that experience leads to adaptation, and past adaptations determine the individual's construction of the meaning of current events. Adaptation, however, is not static. Future experiences can either confirm or disconfirm the meanings attached to them. Disconfirmation will lead to new adaptations.

To conclude: at birth the infant is, biologically, the product of evolutionary adaptation, but he has an individual genotype. His possibilities, while not unlimited, are wide. He will then be exposed to his cultural, social and physical environment so that, by the age of five, he will have developed a predominantly optimistic or pessimistic orientation towards the challenges of life. This may change but not without considerable relearning. The child's characteristic orientation depends on the extent to which his earlier experiences were in a facilitating environment: that is, an environment which developed a belief in the child that he was able to cope with the outer world by helping him to form a meaningful and acceptable inner world. The child who has lived in an impoverished cultural, social or physical environment and is thus emotionally and/or materially deprived has not been specifically deprived, rather he has been generally deprived of his birthright – which is the right to the joy in the present and hope for the future which comes from within.

> Go, said the bird, for the leaves were full of children,
> Hidden excitedly, containing laughter.
> Go, go, go, said the bird: human kind
> Cannot bear very much reality.
> Time past and time future
> What might have been and what has been
> Point to one end which is always present.

>   T.S. Eliot: *Burnt Norton*

Suggestions for further reading

Bower, T.G.R. (1974) *Development in Infancy*. San Francisco: W.H. Freeman.

Bower, T.G.R. (1977) *A Primer of Infant Development*. San Francisco: W.H. Freeman.

Bowlby, J. (1969) *Attachment and Loss*, Vol. 1: *Attachment*. London: Hogarth Press (Pelican Books, 1971).

Bowlby, J. (1973) *Attachment and Loss*, Vol. 2: *Separation Anxiety and Anger*. London: Hogarth Press (Pelican Books, 1975).

Ciba Foundation Symposium 33 (1975) *Parent-Infant Interaction*. Amsterdam: Associated Scientific Publishers.

Clarke, Ann M. and Clarke, A.D.B. (eds) (1976) *Early Experience Myth and Evidence*. London: Open Books.

Donaldson, Margaret (1978) *Children's Minds*. London: Fontana.

Dunn, J.F. (1977) *Distress and Comfort*. London: Fontana/Open Books.

Erikson, Erik H. (1950) *Childhood and Society*. London: Hogarth Press (Penguin Books, 1965).

Freedman, D.G. (1974) *Human Infancy: An Evolutionary Perspective*. New York: Wiley.

Freud, Anna (1937) *The Ego and the Mechanisms of Defence*. London: Hogarth Press.

Garvey, C. (1977) *Play*. London: Fontana/Open Books.

Green, Judith (1975) *Thinking and Language*. London: Methuen.

Jahoda, Marie (1977) *Freud and the Dilemmas of Psychology*. London: Hogarth Press.

Lamb, Michael E. (ed.) (1976) *The Role of the Father in Child Development*. New York: Wiley.

Lewin, R. (ed.) (1975) *Child Alive*. London: Temple Smith.

Lewis, M. and Rosenblum, L.A. (eds) (1974) *The Effect of the Infant on its Caregiver*. New York: Wiley.

Lewis, M. and Rosenblum, A. (eds) (1977) *Interaction, Conversation and the Development of Language*. New York: Wiley.

Lewis, M. and Rosenblum, A. (eds) (1978) *The Development of Affect*. New York: Plenum.

Mahler, M.S., Pine, F. and Bergman, A. (1975) *The Psychological Birth of the Human Infant*. London: Hutchinson.

Murphy, Lois Barclay and Moriarty, Alice E. (1976) *Vulnerability, Coping and Growth*. New Haven: Yale University Press.

Piaget, J. and Inhelder, B. (1969) *The Psychology of the Child*. London: Routledge.

Rutter, M. (1972) *Maternal Deprivation Reassessed.* Harmondsworth: Penguin Books.

Schaffer, H.R. (ed.) (1971) *The Origins of Human Social Relations*. London: Academic Press.

Schaffer, H.R. (ed.) (1977) *Studies in Mother Infant Interaction*. London: Academic Press.

Schaffer, H.R. (1977) *Mothering*. London: Fontana/Open Books.

Segal, Hanna (1979) *Melanie Klein*. London: Fontana.

Smirnoff, V. (1971) *The Scope of Child Analysis*. London: Routledge & Kegan Paul.

Stern, Daniel (1977) *The First Relationship: Infant and Mother*. London: Fontana/Open Books.

Stone, L. Joseph, Smith, Henrietta T. and Murphy, Lois B. (eds) (1974) *The Competent Infant*. London: Tavistock.

Sutton-Smith, Brian and Rosenberg, D.S. (1970) *The Sibling.* New York: Holt, Rinehart & Winston.

Turner, Johanna (1975) *Cognitive Development*. London: Methuen.

Winnicott, D.W. (1958) *Collected Papers*. London: Tavistock.

Winnicott, D.W. (1965) *The Maturational Process and the Facilitating Environment*. London: Hogarth Press.

Wollheim, Richard (1971) *Freud*. London: Fontana.

Yarrow, L.J., Rubenstein, J.L. and Pedersen, F.A. (1975) *Infant and Environment: Early Cognitive and Motivational Development.* Washington, DC: Hemisphere Wiley.

References

Abelin, Ernest L. (1971) The role of the father in the separation-individuation process. In John B. McDevitt and Calvin Settlage (eds) *Separation -Individuation*. New York: International Universities Press.

Altus, W.D. (1962) Sibling order and scholastic aptitude. *American Psychologist 17*: 304.

Ambrose, J.A. (1961) The development of the smiling response in early infancy. In B.M. Foss (ed.) *Determinants of Infant Behaviour*. London: Methuen.

Ban, P. and Lewis, M. (1974) Mothers and fathers, girls and boys: attachment behaviour in the one-year-old. *Merrill Palmer Quarterly 20:* 195-204.

Bates, Elizabeth, Benigni, Laura, Brotherton, Inge, Camaioni, Luigia and Volterra, Virginia (1977) From gesture to the first word: on cognitive and social pre-requisites. In Michael Lewis and Leonard A. Rosenblum (eds) *Interaction, Conversation and the Development of Language.* New York: Wiley.

Baumrind, D. (1967) Effects of authoritative parental control on child behaviour. *Child Development 38:* 888-907.

Bayley, N. and Schaefer, E.S. (1964) Correlations of maternal and child behaviours with the development of mental abilities: data from the Berkeley Growth Study. *Monographs of the Society for Research in Child Development 29*, 6 (Serial No. 97): 1-30.

Bell, S. (1970) The development of the concept of object as related to infant-mother attachment. *Child Development 41:* 291-311.

Bell, S.M. and Ainsworth, M.D.S. (1972) Infant crying and maternal responsiveness. *Child Development 43:* 1171-90.

Benedek, T. (1938) Adaptation to reality in early infancy. *Psychoanalytic Quarterly 7:* 200-14.

Benedek, T. (1956) Toward the biology of the depressive constellation. *Journal of the American Psychoanalytic Association 4:* 389-427.

Bennett, Stephen L. (1971) Infant-caretaker interactions. *Journal of the American Academy of Child Psychiatry 10:* 321-35. Reproduced in Eveoleen N. Rexford, Louis W. Sander and Theodore Shapiro (eds) (1976) *Infant Psychiatry: A New Synthesis.* New Haven: Yale University Press.

Bentovim, A. (1975) Discussion of 'Human maternal behaviour after delivery'. In Ciba Foundation Symposium 33, *Parent-Infant Interaction.* Amsterdam: Associated Scientific Publishers.

Biller, H.B. (1974) *The father-infant relationship: some naturalistic observations.* Unpublished manuscript, University of Rhode Island.

Birns, Beverley (1965) Individual differences in human neonates' responses to stimulation. *Child Development 36:* 249-56.

Bossard, J.H.S. (1945) Family modes of expression. *American Sociological Review 10:* 226-37.

Bossard, J.H.S. and Boll, E. (1960) *The Sociology of Child Development.* New York: Harper & Row.

Bott, E. (1955) Urban families: conjugal roles and social networks. *Human Relations 8:* 345-84.

Bower, T.G.R. (1971) The object in the world of the infant. *Scientific American 225:* 30-8.

Bower, T.G.R. (1974) *Development in Infancy.* San Francisco: W.H. Freeman.

Bower, T.G.R. (1977) *A Primer of Infant Development.* San Francisco: W.H. Freeman.

Bowlby, J. (1961) The Adolf Meyer Lecture: Childhood mourning and its implications for psychiatry. *American Journal of Psychiatry 188:* 481-97.

Bowlby, J. (1969) *Attachment and Loss,* Vol. 1: *Attachment.* London: Hogarth Press (Pelican Books, 1971).

Bowlby, J. (1973) *Attachment and Loss*, Vol. 2: *Separation, Anxiety and Anger.* London: Hogarth Press (Pelican Books, 1975).

Bradley, R. (1963) Father's presence in delivery rooms. *Psychosomatics 3:* 474-9.

Brazelton, T.B. (1975) Discussion of 'Human maternal behaviour after delivery'. In Ciba Foundation Symposium 33, *Parent-Infant Interaction.* Amsterdam: Associated Scientific Publishers.

Brazelton, T. B., Kowlowski, Barbara and Main, Mary (1974) The origins of reciprocity: the early mother-infant interaction. In Michael

Lewis and Leonard A. Rosenblum (eds) *The Effect of the Infant on its Caregiver*. New York: Wiley.

Brody, J. and Axelrad, S. (1971) Maternal stimulation and the social responsiveness of infants. In H.R. Schaffer (ed.) *The Origins of Human Social Relations*. London: Academic Press.

Bronson, G.W. (1962) Critical periods in human development. *British Journal of Medical Psychology 35:* 127-33.

Bronson, G.W. (1970) Fear of visual novelty: developmental patterns in males and females. *Developmental Psychology 2:* 33-40.

Bronson, G.W. (1971) Fear of the unfamiliar in human infants. In H.R. Schaffer (ed.) *The Origins of Human Social Relations*. London: Academic Press.

Bronson, G.W. (1974) Infants' reaction to an unfamiliar person. In L. Joseph Stone, Henrietta T. Smith and Lois B. Murphy (eds) *The Competent Infant*. London: Tavistock.

Bronson, W.C. (1971) The growth of competence: issues of conceptualization and measurement. In H.R. Schaffer (ed.) *The Origins of Human Social Relations*. London: Academic Press.

Brooks, Jeanne and Lewis, Michael (1975) *Person perception and verbal labelling: the development of social labelling*. Paper presented at the meeting of the Society for Research in Child Development, 1975.

Brooks, Jeanne and Lewis, Michael (1976) Infants' response to strangers: midget, adult and child. *Child Development 47:* 323-32.

Brooks, V. and Hochberg, J. (1960) A psychophysical study of 'cuteness'. *Perceptual and Motor Skills 11:* 205.

Brophy, J.E. (1970) Mothers as teachers of their own pre-school children: the influence of sociometric status and task structures on teaching specificity. *Child Development 41:* 79-94.

Bruch, H. (1974) *Eating Disorders: Obesity, Anorexia Nervosa, and the Person Within*. London: Routledge & Kegan Paul.

Bruner, J.S. (1968) *Processes of Cognitive Growth: Infancy*. (Heinz Werner Lecture Series 3). Worcester, Mass.: Clarke University Press/ Barre Publishers. Extracts reproduced in L. Joseph Stone, Henrietta T. Smith and Lois B. Murphy (eds) (1974) *The Competent Infant*. London: Tavistock.

Bruner, J.S. (1972) The nature and uses of immaturity. *American Psychologist 27:* 687-708.

Bruner, J.S. (1974) Nature and uses of immaturity. In Kevin Connolly and Jerome Bruner (eds) *The Growth of Competence*. London: Academic Press.

Bruner, J.S. (1977) Early social interaction and language acquisition. In H.R. Schaffer (ed.) *Studies in Mother-Infant Interaction*. London: Academic Press

Burlingham, D. and Freud, A. (1942) *Young Children in War-Time*. London: Allen & Unwin.

Carpenter, Genevieve (1975) Mother's face and the new born. In Roger Lewin (ed.) *Child Alive*. London: Temple Smith.

Cazden, Courtney B. (1977) The question of intent. In Michael Lewis and Leonard A. Rosenblum (eds) *Interaction, Conversation and the Development of Language*. New York: Wiley.

Chamove, A., Harlow, H. and Mitchell, G. (1967) Sex differences in the infant-directed behaviour of pre-adolescent rhesus monkeys. *Child Development 38:* 329-35.

Chess, Stella (1970) Temperament and children at risk. In E. James Anthony and Cyrille Koupernik (eds) *The Child in his Family*, Vol. 1. New York: Wiley.

Cicchetti, Dante and Sroufe, L. Alan (1978) An organizational view of affect: illustration from the study of Downs Syndrome infants. In Michael Lewis and Leonard A. Rosenblum (eds) *The Development of Affect*. New York: Plenum Press.

Clarke-Stewart, A.K. (1963) Interactions between mothers and their young children: characteristics and consequences. *Monographs of the Society for Research in Child Development 153:* 38, No. 6-7.

Coleman, J.S. et al. (1966) *Equality of Educational Opportunity*. U.S. Dept of Health, Education and Welfare, Office of Education, Washington, DC.

Collis, G.M. and Schaffer, H.R. (1975) Synchronisation of visual attention in mother-infant pairs. *Journal of Child Psychology and Psychiatry 16:* 315-20.

Connolly, Kevin and Bruner, J.S. (1974) Competence: its nature and nurture. In Kevin Connolly and Jerome Bruner (eds) *The Growth of Competence*. London: Academic Press.

Coopersmith, S. (1967) *The Antecedents of Self-Esteem*. San Francisco: W.H. Freeman.

Crandall, V.C., Katkovsky, W. and Crandall, V.J. (1965) Children's beliefs in their own control of reinforcements in intellectual academic achievement situations. *Child Development 36:* 91-109.

Cryan, J. (1968) *Ordinal position and masculinity-femininity. Their influence on female personality*. Masters thesis, Bowling-Green State University.

Cushna, B. (1966) *Agency and birth order differences in very early childhood.* Paper presented at the meeting of the American Psychological Association, New York.

Cytryn, Leon (1968) Methodological issues in psychiatric evaluation of infants. *The Journal of the American Academy of Child Psychiatry 7:* 510-21.

Décarie, Thérèse Gouin (1978) Affect development and cognition in a Piagetian context. In Michael Lewis and Leonard A. Rosenblum (eds) *The Development of Affect.* New York: Plenum.

Devore, Irven and Konner, Melvin J. (1974) Infancy in hunter-gatherer life: an ethological perspective. In Norman F. White (ed.) *Ethology and Psychiatry.* Toronto: University of Toronto Press.

Dolto, F. (1936) *Psychoanalyse et Pédiatrie.* Paris: Editions de la Parole (1961).

Donaldson, Margaret (1978) *Children's Minds.* London: Fontana.

Dore, J. (1973) *On the development of speech acts.* Unpublished doctoral dissertation, University of New York.

Dore, J. (1974) A pragmatic description of early language development. *Journal of Psycholinguistic Research 4.*

Dunn, F. (1975) Consistency and change in styles of mothering. In Ciba Foundation Symposium 33, *Parent-Infant Interaction.* Amsterdam: Associated Scientific Publishers.

Dunn, J.F. (1977a) *Distress and Comfort.* London: Fontana/Open Books.

Dunn, J.F. (1977b) Patterns of interaction: continuities and consequences. In H.R. Schaffer (ed.) *Studies in Mother-Infant Interaction.* London: Academic Press.

Erikson, Erik H. (1950) *Childhood and Society.* New York: Norton (Penguin Books, 1965).

Erikson, Erik H. (1959) Growth and crisis in the healthy personality. *Psychological Issues I:* 50-100.

Escalona, S.K. (1953) Emotional development in the first year of life. In M. Senn (ed.) *Problems of Infancy and Childhood.* New York: Josiah Macy Jr Foundation.

Escalona, S.K. (1968) *The Roots of Individuality: Normal Patterns of Development in Infancy.* Chicago: Aldine Publishing Co.

Fairbairn, W.R.P. (1952) *Psychoanalytic Studies of the Personality.* London: Tavistock.

Feschbach, N.D. (1973) Cross cultural studies of teaching styles in four-year-olds and their mothers. In A.D. Pick (ed.) *Minnesota Symposia on Child Psychology*, Vol. 7. Minneapolis: University of Minnesota Press.

Finneran, M.P. (1958) Dependency and self-concept as functions of acceptance-rejection by others. *American Psychologist 13:* 332.

Fleener, D.E. and Cairns, R.B. (1970) Attachment behaviours in human infants: discriminative vocalization on maternal separation. *Developmental Psychology 2:* 215-23.

Freedle, Roy and Lewis, Michael (1977) Prelinguistic conversations. In Michael Lewis and Leonard A. Rosenblum (eds) *Interaction, Conversation and the Development of Language.* New York: Wiley.

Freedman, D.G. (1974) *Human Infancy: An Evolutionary Perspective.* New York: Wiley.

Freud, Anna (1937) *The Ego and the Mechanisms of Defence.* London: Hogarth Press.

Freud, S. (1897) Letter to Fliess. In Marie Bonaparte, Anna Freud and Ernst Kris (eds) (1954) *The Origins of Psychoanalysis.* New York: Basic Books, p. 223.

Freud, S. (1899) Letter to Fliess. In Marie Bonaparte, Anna Freud and Ernst Kris (eds) (1954) *The Origins of Psychoanalysis.* New York: Basic Books, p. 298.

Freud, S. (1905) *Three Essays on the Theory of Sexuality.* Standard Edition, Vol. 7. London: Hogarth Press.

Freud, S. (1910) *A Special Type of Object Choice.* Standard Edition, Vol. 24. London: Hogarth Press.

Freud, S. (1915a) *Instincts and their Vicissitudes.* Standard Edition, Vol. 14. London: Hogarth Press.

Freud, S. (1915b) *The Unconscious.* Standard Edition, Vol. 14. London: Hogarth Press.

Freud, S. (1916) *Introductory Lectures.* Standard Edition, Vol. 14. London: Hogarth Press.

Freud, S. (1921) *Group Psychology and the Analysis of the Ego.* Standard Edition, Vol. 18. London: Hogarth Press.

Freud, S. (1923) *The Ego and the Id.* Standard Edition, Vol. 19. London: Hogarth Press.

Freud, S. (1924) *The Dissolution of the Oedipus Complex.* Standard Edition, Vol. 19. London: Hogarth Press.

Freud, S. (1926a) *The Question of Lay Analysis.* Standard Edition, Vol. 20. London: Hogarth Press.

Freud, S. (1926b) *Inhibitions, Symptoms and Anxiety.* Standard Edition, Vol. 20, London: Hogarth Press.

Freud, S. (1929) *Civilization and its Discontents.* Standard Edition, Vol. 21, London: Hogarth Press.

Freud, S. (1932) 'Femininity'. *New Introductory Lectures*, Lecture 33. Standard Edition, Vol. 22, London: Hogarth Press.

Freud, S. (1937) *Analysis Terminable and Interminible.* Standard Edition, Vol. 23, London: Hogarth Press.

Freud, S. (1940) *An Outline of Psycho-analysis.* Standard Edition, Vol. 23, London: Hogarth Press.

Fries, Margaret E. and Woolf, Paul J. (1971) The influence of constitutional complex on developmental phases. In John B. McDevitt and Calvin F. Settlage (eds) *Separation-Individuation.* New York: International Universities Press.

Fuller, G.B., Zarrow, M.X. Anderson, C.O. and Denenberg, V.H. (1970) Testosterone propionate during gestation in the rabbit: effect on subsequent maternal behaviour. *Journal of Reproduction and Fertility 23:* 285-90.

Garvey, C. (1977) *Play.* London: Fontana/Open Books.

Gesell, A. and Ames, L.B. (1937) Early evidence of individuality in the human infant. *Scientific Monthly 45:* September 1939: 217-25.

Gewirtz, J.L. (1948) *Succorance in young children.* Ph.D. thesis, State University of Iowa, Iowa City.

Gewirtz, J.L. (1961) ' Learning analysis of the effects of normal stimulation, privation, and deprivation on the acquisition of social motivation and attachment. In B.M. Foss (ed.) *Determinants of Infant Behaviour.* London: Methuen.

Gilbert, G.M. (1970) *Personality Dynamics: A Biosocial Approach.* New York: Harper & Row.

Gill, D.G. (1970) *Violence Against Children.* Cambridge, Mass.: Harvard University Press.

Glidewell, John C. (1961) *Parental Attitudes and Child Behaviour.* Springfield, Illinois: Charles C. Thomas.

Golding, William (1959) *Free Fall.* London: Faber.

Greenberg, M. and Morris, N. (1974) The newborn's impact upon the father. *American Journal of Orthopsychiatry 44:* 520-1.

Guntrip, Harry (1968) *Schizoid Phenomena, Object Relations and the Self.* London: Hogarth Press.

Haan, Norma (1977) *Coping and Defending. Processes of Self Environment Organization.* New York: Academic Press.

Halliday, M. (1975) *Learning How to Mean: Explorations in the Development of Language.* London: Arnold.

Heider, Grace M. (1966) Vulnerability in infants and young children. A pilot study. *Genetic Psychology Monographs*, vols. 73-4.

Heinicke, C.M. and Westheimer, I.J. (1965) *Brief Separations*. London: Longman.

Hess, R.D. and Shipman, V.C. (1965) Early experience and the socialization of cognitive modes in children. *Child Development* 36, 869-86.

Hess, R.D. and Shipman, V.C. (1967) Cognitive elements in maternal behaviour. In J.P. Hill (ed.) *Minnesota Symposia on Child Psychology*, Vol. 1. Minneapolis: University of Minnesota Press.

Hilton, I. (1967) Differences in the behaviour of mothers toward first and later born children. *Journal of Personality and Social Psychology 7:* 282-90.

Hinde, R.A. (1972) Mother-infant separation in rhesus monkeys. *Nature 239:* 41-2.

Hinde, R.A. and Spencer-Booth, Y. (1970) Individual differences in responses of Rhesus monkeys to a period of separation from their mothers. *Journal of Child Psychology and Psychiatry 11:* 159-76.

Home, H.J. (1966) The concept of mind. *International Journal of Psycho-Analysis 47:* 42-9.

Hudson, Liam (1966) *Contrary Imaginations*. London: Methuen.

Hutt, C. (1967) Effects of stimulus novelty on manipulative exploration in an infant. *Journal of Child Psychology and Psychiatry 8:* 241-7.

Jacobs, Martin A. et al. (1972) Parent-child relationships and illness behaviour. *Journal of Consulting and Clinical Psychology 39:* 49-55.

Jahoda, Marie (1977) *Freud and the Dilemmas of Psychology*. London: Hogarth Press.

Kagan, J. (1971) Discussion of fear of the unfamiliar in human infants. In R.H. Schaffer (ed.) *The Origins of Human Social Relations*. London: Academic Press.

Kalnins, J. and Bruner, J. (1973) The co-ordination of visual observation and instrumental behaviour in early infancy. *Perception 2:* 307-14.

Katkovsky, V.C., Crandall, V.C. and Good, S. (1967) Parental antecedents of children's beliefs in internal-external control of reinforcements in intellectual achievement situations. *Child Development 38:* 765-76.

Kaufman, I.C. (1974) Mother/infant relations in monkeys and humans: a reply to Professor Hinde. In Norman F. White (ed.) *Ethology and Psychiatry*. Toronto: University of Toronto Press.

Kaufman, I.C. and Rosenblum, L.A. (1966) A behavioural taxonomy of

M. Nemestrina and M. Radiata; based on longitudinal observations of family groups in the laboratory. *Primates* 7: 205-58.

Kaufman, I.C. and Rosenblum, L.A. (1969) The waning of the mother-infant bond in two species of macaque. In B.M. Foss (ed.) *Determinants of Infant Behaviour*, Vol. 4. London: Methuen.

Kaye, Kenneth (1977) Toward the origin of dialogue. In H.R. Schaffer (ed.) *Studies in Mother Infant Interaction*. London: Academic Press.

Kendon, A. (1967) Some functions of gaze direction in social interaction. *Acta Psychologica 26:* 22-63.

Klaus, Marshall H., Trause, Mary Ann and Kennell, John H. (1975) Does human maternal behaviour after delivery show a characteristic pattern? In Ciba Foundation Symposium 33, *Parent-Infant Interaction.* Amsterdam: Associated Scientific Publishers.

Klein, M. (1932) *The Psychoanalysis of Children*. London: Hogarth.

Kluckholm, Clyde and Murray, Henry A. (eds) (1971) *Personality in Nature, Society and Culture*, 2nd edn. New York: Alfred A. Knopf.

Koch, H.L. (1954) The relation of 'primary mental abilities' in five- and six-year-olds to sex of child and characteristics of his siblings. *Child Development 25:* 209-23.

Koch, H.L. (1955) Some personality correlates of sex, sibling position and sex of sibling among five- and six-year-old children. *Genetic Psychological Monographs 52:* 3-50.

Koch, H.L. (1956) Some emotional attitudes of young children in relation to characteristics of his sibling. *Child Development 27:* 393-426.

Korner, A.F. (1964) Some hypotheses regarding the significance of individual differences at birth for later development. *Psychoanalytic Study of the Child 19:* 58-72.

Korner, A.F. (1971) Individual differences at birth: implications for early experience and later development. *American Journal of Orthopsychiatry 41:* 608-19.

Korner, A.F. and Grobstein, R. (1967) Individual differences at birth. Implications for mother-infant relationship and later development. *Journal of the American Academy of Child Psychiatry 6:* 676-90. Reproduced in Eveoleen N. Rexford, Louis W. Sander and Theodore Shapiro (eds) (1976) *Infant Psychiatry: A New Synthesis*. New Haven: Yale University Press.

Korner, A.F. and Thoman, E.B. (1970) Visual alertness in neonates as evoked by maternal care. *Journal of Experimental Child Psychology 10:* 67-78.

Korner, A.F. and Thoman, E.B. (1972) The relative efficacy of contact and vestibular-proprioceptive stimulation in soothing neonates. *Child Development 43:* 443-53.

Kotelchuck, M. (1972) *The nature of the child's tie to his father.* Unpublished doctoral dissertation, Harvard University.

Kotelchuck, M. (1976) The infant's relationship to the father: experimental evidence. In Michael E. Lamb (ed.) *The Role of the Father in Child Development.* New York: Wiley.

Lamb, Michael E. (1976) Interactions between eight-month-old children and their fathers and mothers. In Michael E. Lamb (ed.) *The Role of the Father in Child Development.* New York: Wiley.

Lawick-Goodall, Jane van (1971) *In the Shadow of Man.* London: William Collins.

Lawrence, D.H. (1915) *The Rainbow.* London: Methuen (Penguin edn. 1949).

Lewis, M. and Brooks, J. (1978) Self knowledge and emotional development. In Michael Lewis and Leonard Rosenblum (eds) *The Development of Affect.* New York: Plenum Press.

Lewis, M. and McGurk, H. (1972) Evaluation of infant intelligence. *Science 178:* 1174-7.

Lewis, M. and Weinraub, M. (1976) The father's role in the child's social network. In Michael E. Lamb (ed.) *The Role of the Father in Child Development.* New York: Wiley.

MacFarlane, J.Aidan (1975) A faction in the development of social preferences in the human neonate. In Ciba Foundation Symposium 33, *Parent Infant Interaction.* Amsterdam, Associated Scientific Publishers.

MacFarlane, J. Aidan, (1977) *The Psychology of Childbirth.* London: Fontana/Open Books.

MacFarlane, J.W. (1964) Perspectives on personality consistency and change from the guidance study. *Vita Humana 7:* 115-25.

Madison, Peter (1961) *Freud's Concept of Repression and Defence, its Theoretical and Observational Language.* Minneapolis: University of Minnesota Press.

Mahler, Margaret S. (1952) On child psychosis and schizophrenia: autistic and symbiotic infantile psychoses. *The Psychoanalytic Study of the Child 7:* 286-305.

Mahler, Margaret S. (1965a) On early infantile psychosis. *Journal of the American Academy of Child Psychiatry 4:* 554-68. Reproduced in Eveoleen N. Rexford, Louis W. Sander and Theodore Shapiro (eds)

(1976)*Infant Psychiatry: A New Synthesis.* New Haven: Yale University Press.

Mahler, Margaret S. (1965b) On the significance of the normal separation-individuation phase. In M. Schur (ed.) *Drives, Affects and Behaviour*, vol. 2. New York: International Universities Press.

Mahler, Margaret S. (1968) *On Human Symbiosis and the Vicissitudes of Individuation.* New York: International University Press.

Mahler, Margaret S., Pine, Fred, and Bergman, Anni (1975) *The Psychological Birth of the Human Infant.* London: Hutchison.

McCall, R.B. and Garratt, C.R. (1971)*Qualitative aspects of exploratory behaviour in infants.* Unpublished ms.

McGhee, P.E. and Crandall, U.C. (1968) Beliefs in internal-external control of reinforcements and academic performance. *Child Development 39:* 91-102.

Mead, G.H. (1934) *Mind, Self and Society.* Chicago: University of Chicago Press.

Mehrabian, A. (1972) *Nonverbal Communication.* New York: Aldine Atherton.

Milne, A.A. (1927)*Now We Are Six.* London: Methuen.

Money, J. and Ehrhardt, A.A. (1972)*Man and Woman, Boy and Girl.* Baltimore: Johns Hopkins University Press.

Monnier, C. (1976)*La genèse de l'experimentation: exploration d'objets nouveaux par les bébés.* Doctoral dissertation, University of Geneva.

Morgan, George A. and Ricciuti, Henry N. (1969)Infants' responses to strangers during the first year. In B.M. Foss (ed.) *Determinants of Infant Behaviour*, vol. 4. London: Methuen.

Moss, H.A. (1967) Sex, age and state as determinants of mother-infant interaction. *Merrill-Palmer Quarterly 13:* 19-36.

Mundy-Castle, A.C. and Anglin, J. (1969) *The development of looking in infancy.* Paper presented at conference of the Society for Research in Child Development, Santa Monica, California.

Murphy, Lois Barclay (1962) *The Widening World of Childhood: Paths Toward Mastery.* New York: Basic Books.

Murphy, Lois Barclay (1974) Coping, vulnerability and resilience in childhood. In George U. Coelho, David A. Hamburg and John E. Adams (eds) *Coping and Adaptation.* New York: Basic Books.

Murphy, Lois Barclay and Moriarty, Alice E. (1976) *Vulnerability, Coping and Growth.* New Haven: Yale University Press.

Newson, John and Newson, Elizabeth (1976) On the social origins of symbolic functioning. In P. Varma and Phillip Williams (eds)

Piaget, Psychology and Education. London: Hodder and Stoughton.

Papoušek, H. (1967) Experimental studies of appetitional behaviour in human new borns and infants. In H.W. Stevenson et al. (eds) *Early Behaviour: Comparative and Developmental Approaches*. New York: Wiley.

Papoušek, H. (1969) Individual variability in learned responses in human infants. In R.J. Robinson (ed.) *Brain and Early Behaviour*. London: Academic Press.

Papoušek, H. and Papoušek, M. (1975) Cognitive aspects of preverbal social interaction between human infants and adults. In Ciba Foundation Symposium 33, *Parent-Infant Interaction*. Amsterdam: Associated Scientific Publishers.

Papousek, H. and Papoušek, M. (1977) Mothering and the cognitive head start: psychobiological considerations. In H.R. Schaffer (ed.) *Studies in Mother-Infant Interaction*. London: Academic Press.

Paraskevopoulos, J. and Hunt, McV. (1971) 'Object construction and imitation under differing conditions of rearing. *Journal of Genetic Psychology 119:* 301.

Parke, R.D. and O'Leary, S. (1975) Father-mother-infant interaction in the newborn period: some findings, some observations and some unresolved issues. In K. Riegiel and J. Meacham (eds) *The Developing Individual in a Changing World*, Vol. 2 *Social and Environmental Issues*. The Hague: Mouton.

Pedersen, F.A. and Robson, K.S. (1969) Father participation in infancy. *American Journal of Orthopsychiatry 39:* 466-72.

Piaget, J. (1930) *The Child's Conception of Physical Causality*. London: Routledge & Kegan Paul.

Piaget, J. (1951) *Play, Dreams and Imitation in Childhood*. London: Routledge & Kegan Paul.

Piaget, J. (1952) *The Origins of Intelligence in Children*. New York: International Universities Press.

Piaget, J. (1954) *The Construction of Reality in the Child*. New York: Basic Books.

Piaget, J. and Inhelder, B. (1969) *The Psychology of the Child*. New York: Basic Books.

Pine, F. (1971) On the separation process: universal trends and individual differences. In John B. McDevitt and Calvin F. Settlage *Separation Individuation*. New York: International Universities Press.

Provence, Sally (1978) A clinician's view of affect development in infancy. In Michael Lewis and Leonard A. Rosenblum (eds) *The Development of Affect*. New York: Plenum.

Radin, Norma (1976) The role of the father in cognitive, academic and intellectual development. In Michael E. Lamb (ed.) *The Role of the Father in Child Development.* New York: Wiley.

Redshaw, M. and Hughes, J. (1975) *Cognitive development in primate infancy.* Paper presented to the 137th annual meeting of the British Association for the Advancement of Science, University of Surrey.

Rheingold, H.L. (1969) The effect of a strange environment on the behaviour of infants. In B.M. Foss (ed.) *Determinants of Infant Behaviour,* Vol. 4. London: Methuen.

Rheingold, H.L. and Eckerman, C.O. (1969) The infant's free entry into a new environment. *Journal of Experimental Child Psychology 8:* 271-83.

Rheingold, H.L. and Eckerman, C.O. (1971) Departure from the mother. In H.R. Schaffer (ed.) *The Origins of Human Social Relations.* London: Academic Press.

Rheingold, H.L., Gewirtz, J.L. and Ross, A.W. (1959) Social conditioning of vocalizations in the infant. *Journal of Comparative Physiological Psychology 52:* 68-73.

Robertson, J. (1952) *A Two-Year-Old goes to Hospital* (16 mm. sound film with guidebook). Tavistock Child Development Research Unit.

Robertson, J. and Bowlby, J. (1952) Responses of young children to separation from their mothers. *Courrier de la Centre Internationale de l'Enfance* Vol. 2, 131-42.

Robertson, J. and Robertson, J. (1967) *Young Children in brief separation: I. Kate, aged 2 years 5 months in fostercare for 27 days.* Tavistock Child Development Research Unit.

Robertson, J. and Robertson, J. (1968a) *Young Children in brief separation: 2. Jane, aged 17 months in fostercare for 10 days.* Tavistock Child Development Research Unit.

Robertson, J. and Robertson, J. (1968b) *Young Children in brief separation: 3. John, aged 17 months 9 days in a residential nursery.* Tavistock Child Development Research Unit.

Rosenberg, B.G. and Sutton-Smith, B. (1964) The relationship of ordinal position and sibling sex status to cognitive abilities. *Psychonomic Science 1:* 81-2.

Rosenberg, B.G. and Sutton-Smith, B. (1966) Sibling association, family size and cognitive abilities. *Journal of Genetic Psychology 109:* 271-9.

Rosenblum, Leonard A. (1971) Infant attachment in monkeys. In H.R. Schaffer (ed.) *The Origins of Human Social Relations.* London: Academic Press.

Rosenblum, Leonard A. and Youngstein, Kenneth P. (1974) Developmental changes in compensatory dyadic response in mother and infant monkeys. In Michael A. Lewis and Leonard Rosenblum (eds) *The Effect of the Infant on its Caregiver.* New York: Wiley.

Ross, H.S. (1972) *Novelty and complexity as determinants of exploratory behaviour in 12-month-old infants.* Unpublished dissertation, University of North Carolina.

Rothbart, M.L. (1967) Birth order and mother-child interaction. Doctoral dissertation, Stanford University. Ann Arbor, Mich: Michigan University Microfilms No 67-7961.

Rutter, M. (1971) Parent-child separation: psychological effects on the children. *Journal of Child Psychology and Psychiatry 12:* 233-60.

Rutter, M. (1972) *Maternal Deprivation Reassessed.* Harmondsworth: Penguin Books.

Saarni, Carolyn (1978) Cognitive and communicative features of emotional experience, or Do you show what you think you feel? In Michael Lewis and Leonard A. Rosenblum (eds) *The Development of Affect.* New York: Plenum Press.

Salter-Ainsworth, Mary D., Bell, Sylvia M.V., Stayton, Donelda J. (1971) Individual differences in strange situation behaviour of one-year-olds. In H.R. Schaffer (ed.) *The Origins of Human Social Relations.* London: Academic Press.

Sander, L.W. (1962) Issues in early mother-child interaction. *Journal of the American Academy of Child Psychiatry 1:* 144-66.

Sander, L.W. (1969) Comments on regulation and organization in the early infant-caretaker system. In R.J. Robinson (ed.) *Brain and Early Behaviour.* New York: Academic Press.

Sartre, Jean-Paul (1948) *Existentialism and Humanism.* London: Methuen.

Scarr, Sandra and Salapatek, Philip (1970) Patterns of fear development during infancy. *Merrill-Palmer Quarterly 16:* 53-90.

Scarr-Salapatek, Sandra (1976) An evolutionary perspective on infant intelligence: species patterns and individual variations. In Michael Lewis (ed.) *Origins of Intelligence: Infancy and Early Childhood.* London: Wiley.

Schachter, S. (1964) Birth order and sociometric choice. *Journal of Abnormal and Social Psychology 68:* 453-56.

Schaffer, H.R. (1966) The onset of fear of strangers and the incongruity hypothesis. *Journal of Child Psychology and Psychiatry 7:* 95-106.

Schaffer, H.R. (1971a) Cognitive structure and early social behaviour. In H.R. Schaffer (ed.) *The Origins of Human Social Relations.* London: Academic Press.

Schaffer, H.R. (1971b) The nature and development of fear. General discussion in H.R. Schaffer (ed.) *The Origins of Human Social Relations*. London: Academic Press.

Schaffer, H.R. and Emerson, P.E. (1964a) The development of social attachments in infancy. *Monograph of the Society for Research in Child Development*, Vol. 29, No. 3.

Schaffer, H.R. and Emerson, P.E. (1964b) Patterns of response to physical contact in early human development. *Journal of Child Psychology and Psychiatry 5:* 1-13.

Schaffer, H.R. and Parry, M.H. (1970) The effects of short-term familiarization on infants' perceptual-motor co-ordination in a simultaneous discrimination situation. *British Journal of Psychology 61:* 559-69.

Schooler, C. and Caudill, C. (1964) Symptomatology in Japanese and American schizophrenics. *Ethnology 2:* 172-8.

Schoonover, S.M. (1959) The relationship of intelligence and achievement to birth order, sex of sibling, and age interval. *Journal of Educational Psychology 50:* 143-6.

Siegelman, Marvin (1966) Loving and punishing parental behaviour and introversion tendencies in sons. *Child Development 37:* 985-92.

Simonds, P.E. (1974) Sex differences in Bonnet Macaque networks and social structure. *Archives of Sexual Behaviour 3:* 151-66.

Slater, Philip E. (1962) Parental behaviour and personality of the child. *Journal of Genetic Psychology 101:* 53-68.

Snyder, P.A. (1972) Behaviour of *Leontopithecus Rosalia* (The Golden Lion Marmoset) and related species: a review. In D.D. Bridgewater (ed.) *Saving the Lion Marmoset*. Wheeling, West Virginia: The Wild Animal Propagation Trust.

Solomon, R. and Décarie, T. (1976) Fear of strangers: a developmental millstone or an overstudied phenomenon? *Canadian Journal of Behavioral Science 8*(4): 351-63.

Soto, R. (1937) ¿Por qué en la casa de cuna no hay dispepsia transitoria? *Rev. Mex. de Puericultura 8.*

Spelke, E., Zelazo, P, Kagan, J. and Kotelchuck, M. (1973) Father interaction and separation protest. *Developmental Psychology 9:* 83-90.

Spitz, René A. (1959) *A Genetic Field Theory of Ego Formation.* New York: International Universities Press.

Spitz, René A. (1965) *The First Year of Life.* New York: International Universities Press.

Spitz, René A. (1964) The derailment of dialogue: stimulus overload, action cycles and the completion gradient. *Journal of the American Psychoanalytic Association 12:* 752-75.

Spitz, René A. and Wolf, Katherine M. (1946) Anaclitic depression: an inquiry into the genesis of psychiatric conditions in early childhood. *Psychoanalytic Study of the Child 2*, 313-42. Reproduced in L. Joseph Stone, Henrietta T. Smith and Lois B. Murphy (eds) (1974) *The Competent Infant*. London: Tavistock.

Sprince, M. (1972) Die Psychoanalytische Behandlung eines pseudo-debilen hoch intelligenten Jungen mit abnormen Verhaltensweisen. In E. Geleerd (ed.) *Kinderanalytiker bei der Arbeit*. Stuttgart: Ernst Klett.

Stayton, D.J. and Ainsworth, M.D.S. (1973) Individual differences in infant response to brief everyday separations and related to other infant and maternal behaviours. *Developmental Psychology 9:* 226-35.

Stendler, C.B. (1954) Possible causes of overdependency in young children. *Child Development, 25:* 125-46.

Stern, Daniel G. (1974) Mother and infant play: the dyadic interaction involving facial, vocal and gaze behaviours. In Michael Lewis and Leonard A. Rosenblum (eds) *The Effect of the Infant on its Caregiver.* New York: Wiley.

Stern, Daniel G. (1977) *The First Relationship: Infant and Mother.* London: Fontana/Open Books.

Stevens, A.G. (1971) Attachment behaviour, separation anxiety and stranger anxiety in polymatrically reared infants. In H.R. Schaffer (ed.) *The Origins of Human Social Relations*. London: Academic Press.

Stoller, Robert J. (1968) Sex and Gender. London: Hogarth Press.

Stotland, E. and Dunn, R.E. (1962) Identification, opposition, authority, self-esteem and birth order. *Psychological Monographs 76:* (whole no. 528).

Stotland, E. and Dunn, R.E. (1963) Empathy, self-esteem and birth order. *Journal of Abnormal and Social Psychology 66:* 532-40.

Stout, A.M. (1960) *Parent behaviour toward children of differing ordinal position and sibling status.* Unpublished Ph.D. dissertation, University of California, Berkeley.

Sugiyama, Y. (1971) Characteristics of the social life of Bonnet Macaques (*Macaca radiata*). *Primates 12:* 247-66.

Suttie, I.D. (1935) *The Origins of Love and Hate*. London: Kegan Paul.

Sutton-Smith, B. and Rosenberg, B.G. (1966) The dramatic sibling. *Psychological Report 22:* 993-4.

Sutton-Smith, B. and Rosenberg, B.G. (1970) *The Sibling.* New York: Holt, Rinehart & Winston.

Thoman, Evelyn (1975) How a rejective baby affects mother-infant synchrony. In Ciba Foundation Symposium 33, *Parent-Infant Interaction*. Amsterdam: Associated Scientific Publishers.

Thoman, E., Barnett, C., Leiderman, H. and Turner, A. (1970) Neonate-mother interaction: effects of parity on feeding behaviour. *Child Development, 41:* 1103-11.

Thoman, E., Barnett, C. and Leiderman, P. (1971) Feeding behaviours in newborn infants as a function of parity of the mother. *Child Development, 42:* 1471-83.

Thoman, E., Leiderman, P. and Olson (1972) Neonate-mother interaction during breast feeding. *Development Psychology 6:* 110-18.

Thomas, A., Chess, S., Birch, H.G., Hertzig, M.E. and Korn, S. (1963) *Behavioural Individuality in Early Childhood.* New York: New York University Press.

Thomas, A., Chess, S. and Birch, H.G. (1968) *Temperament and Behaviour Disorders in Children.* New York: New York University Press.

Tinbergen, N. (1951) *The Study of Instinct.* London. Oxford University Press.

Tinklepaugh, O.L. and Hartman, C.G. (1937) Behaviour aspects of parturition in the monkey *(Macacus rhesus). Comparative Psychology 11:* 63-98.

Tizard, Barbara and Rees, Judith (1974) A comparison of the effects of adoption, restoration to the natural mother, and continued institutionalization on the cognitive development of four-year-old children. *Child Development 45:* 92-9.

Tizard, Jack and Tizard, Barbara (1971) The social development of two-year-old children in residential nurseries. In H.R. Schaffer (ed.) *The Origins of Human Social Relations.* London: Academic Press.

Trevarthan, C. (1977) Descriptive analyses of infant communicative behaviour. In H.R. Schaffer (ed.) *Studies in Mother Infant Interaction.* London: Academic Press.

Trivers, R.L. (1972) Parental investment and sexual selection. In B. Campbell (ed.) *Sexual Selection and the Descent of Man, 1871-1971.* Chicago: Aldine.

Wahler, R.G. (1967) Infant social attachments: a reinforcement-theory interpretation and investigation. *Child Development 38:* 1079-88.

Washburn, S.L. and Hamburg, P.A. (1965) The implications of primate research. In I. Devore (ed.) *Primate Behaviour.* New York: Holt, Rinehart & Winston.

West, Mary Maxwell and Konner, Melvin J. (1976) The role of the father: an anthropological perspective. In Michael E. Lamb (ed.) *The Role of the Father in Child Development*. New York: Wiley.

White, R.W. (1960) Competence and the psychosexual stages of development. In M.R. Jones (ed.) *Nebraska Symposium on Motivation*. University of Nebraska Press.

Whiting, J.W.M. and Whiting, B.B. (1975) Aloofness and intimacy of husbands and wives – a cross-cultural study. *Ethos 3:* 183-207.

Wickes, Frances G. (1927) *The Inner World of Childhood*. London: Coventure.

Winnicott, D.W. (1945) Primitive emotional development *International Journal of Psychoanalysis 25* and *Collected Papers* (1958). London: Tavistock.

Winnicott, D.W. (1952) Psychosis and child care. *British Journal of Medical Psychology 25* and *Collected Papers* (1958). London: Tavistock.

Winnicott, D.W. (1955) The depressive position in normal emotional development. *British Journal of Medical Psychology* 28: 89-100 and *Collected Papers* (1958). London: Tavistock.

Winnicott, D.W. (1958) Primary maternal preoccupation in *Collected Papers* (1958) London: Tavistock, 300-5.

Winnicott, D.W. (1965) From dependence sensori-motors independence in the development of the individual. In *The Maturational Process and the Facilitating Environment*. London: Hogarth Press.

Wolberg, Lewis R. (1944) The character structure of the rejected child. *Nervous Child 3:* 74-88.

Wolff, Peter, H. (1963) Developmental and motivational concepts in Piaget's sensorimotor theory of intelligence. *Journal of the American Academy of Child Psychiatry 2:* 225-43.

Yarrow, Leon J. (1964) Personality consistency and change: an overview of some conceptual and methodological issues. *Vita Humana 7:* 67-72.

Yarrow, L.J., Rubenstein, J.L. and Pedersen, F.A. (1975) *Infant and Environment: Early Cognitive and Motivational Development*. Washington DC: Hemisphere/Wiley.

Name index

Subject index